Landscaping and the Small Garden

Landscaping and the Small Garden

BY MARJORIE J. DIETZ

DOUBLEDAY & COMPANY, INC.,
GARDEN CITY, NEW YORK

We are indebted to the following for the color plates in this volume:

Plate 1, 2, 5, 6, 10 — Roche
Plate 3, 4, 7, 8, 9, 11, 12, 13 — Marjorie J. Dietz

We are indebted to the following for the black-and-white photographs in this volume:

Page 5, 8, 12, 31, 58, 70, 85, 135, 154 — Helen S. Witty
Page 6, 7 (top and bottom), 10, 22, 38, 47, 53, 63, 64, 66, 68, 81, 106, 110, 119, 121, 123, 127, 128, 129, 144, 145, 146, 148, 156 — Marjorie J. Dietz
Page 15 — Photo by Molly Adams, landscape architect Alice Irey

Page 30, 40, 80, 141 — Margaret Ohlander
Page 42, 87, 94, 140, 157, 162 — George Taloumis
Page 59 — Photo by Western Wood Products Association, landscape architect Daryl B. May

Page 73, 92, 150 — Arthur Norman Orans
Page 76, 78, 82 — Western Wood Products Association
Page 77 — Bellingrath Gardens
Page 89 — The Garden Library, Dumbarton Oaks
Page 136 — Pan American Seeds

Copyright © 1973 by Marjorie J. Dietz

Copyright © 1970 by Nelson Doubleday, Inc.
Garden City, New York
All Rights Reserved
Printed in the United States of America

Contents

INTRODUCTION   1

1. LOOKING AT YOUR LAND   3

    When You Are Building • Protecting Trees from Mechanical Injury • Earth Moving and Topsoil • When the Builder Supplies the Landscaping • Adapting Planting Ideas to Site and Climate • Outdoor Housekeeping: The Problems of Upkeep • The Second Home • Space for Family Essentials and Interests • The Matter of Passage — Walks and Paths • Putting Your Plan on Paper • A Few Guidelines for Basic Landscaping • What to Expect from Landscape Architects or Nurseries

2. PARTS OF THE LANDSCAPE   21

    Start with a Lawn • What Grass Requires • Notes on Popular Grasses • Soil Preparation for Seeding • Planting the Seed • Pointers on Mowing • The Importance of Maintaining Fertility • Renovating an Old Lawn • Laying Sod for an "Instant" Lawn • The Use of Ground Covers • Temporary Ground-cover Plants for One-season Color • Ground Covers for Permanence • Small Trees for Small Properties • Trees for Shade and Ornament • Shrubs for Beauty and Low Maintenance • Broad-leaved Evergreens • Rhododendrons and Evergreen Azaleas • Lists of Shrubs with Special Characteristics and for Special Uses • Planning for Privacy • The Best of the Hedge Plants • Vines and Vine-like Plants • Vines for Modern Gardens • How Important Are Foundation Plantings? • The Area Beyond the Picture Window • Dooryard and Entry Gardens

3. OUTDOOR LIVING AREAS: THE TERRACE OR PATIO   75

   Shape and Size of Terraces • Paving for Patios or Terraces • Shade, Screens, and Overhead Protection • Architectural Features, Decorations, and Accessories • Accent Plants for Pots and Tubs • City Terraces, Gardens, and Window Boxes

4. TIPS FOR EASIER MAINTENANCE   97

   Mowing Strips • A Tool house for Storage • Basic Tools • Mulches and Mulching • Underground Sprinkling System • Work-saving Plants • Coping with Pests • Organic Gardening Methods

5. IDEAS FOR FLOWER GARDENS   107

   Requirements and Locations for Flower Gardens • Permanent Color from Perennials • Suggestions for Flower Garden Color from Spring to Fall • Temporary Color with Annuals and Summer Bulbs • Ten Major Annuals for Reliable, Long-season Color • Hardy Spring-flowering Bulbs for Generous Color with Little Effort • Ten Hardy Bulbs for Spring and Summer • Flower Color in the Shade

6. GARDENS OF SPECIAL PLANTS AND
   FOR SPECIAL INTERESTS   125

   Herb Gardening • The Wild-flower Garden • Vegetables and the Small Garden • A Formal Garden for Vegetables and Herbs • Fruit-yielding Gardens • Pools and Water Gardens • Gardens of Roses • Winter Garden Effects • A List of Plants to Consider for Effectiveness in Winter

7. SMALL GARDEN IDEAS AND PLANT COMBINATIONS   151
   SUGGESTED BOOKS FOR FURTHER REFERENCE   164
   INDEX   166

Introduction

One of the most exciting times in the life of most people is the planning or purchasing of a new home. Whether the house is built to specifications or purchased from a builder, the experience is basically the same — an opportunity to improve upon or refresh living patterns and to express creativity in one's daily existence in new surroundings. New homeowners who have had no previous concern or experience with landscaping and garden maintenance are often frustrated by problems associated with the outside of the house — the front yard open to public scrutiny, plantings around the house, the lawn, a terrace or patio, flower gardens — the entire landscaping of the property. Where to begin?

It is hoped that *Landscaping and the Small Garden* will answer this question for new homeowners as well as for those who have purchased a not-so-new house surrounded by unfamiliar plantings which may need renovation or special attention. But *Landscaping and the Small Garden* is also intended for others, including those who may be embarking on their first — or nearly first — gardening adventures, along with more experienced gardeners who are searching for new ways and ideas to improve their outdoor surroundings. This is not intended to be a how-to-grow-each-plant book, although many such suggestions are included. There are many books which give helpful information on gardening principles in general or which emphasize a particular plant group and how it should be grown. (Some of these books are listed on pages 164–65.)

I would like to express my appreciation to Rachel Snyder, editor-in-chief of *Flower and Garden,* for giving permission to use portions of my articles on broad-leaved evergreens and wild-flower gardening, which originally appeared in that magazine.

Marjorie J. Dietz

1 Looking at Your Land

When you are building

Let's assume that you have purchased a piece of property, a "lot," and have chosen a house design and a builder who is about to begin. If trees exist on the property, the time to protect them during the building process begins before cellar digging and any land clearing. Whether your property has one tree or dozens, their existence is a blessing and means your landscaping has already begun. A brand-new house always appears more at home on its site when set off by existing trees. No matter if one is a crooked old apple tree — the final remnant of a former orchard — or if the trees are a haphazard grove of evergreens such as red-cedars, which are common natives over many regions of this country.

Unless existing trees are in the way of the actual building site, consider them valuable. They can save you money and almost always can be incorporated into later landscaping schemes. The old apple tree, after corrective pruning to remove dead and crowded branches, will take on the special character that is possessed only by an ancient tree, providing blossoms in spring, some shade in summer, and perhaps even a basket of fruit in the fall. The red-cedar grove can become a background for other plantings and, because it is evergreen, can be of year-long interest. In any case, the property with existing trees puts the owners years ahead in comparison with plantings made after the house is completed.

Protecting trees from mechanical injury

There are only a few ways to protect trees during bulldozing and building operations, and obviously you must discuss the problem with your

4   Landscaping and the Small Garden

builder. The trees must be marked, but more important will be physical barriers set up to protect the trunks from serious gougings and other injuries, which can be rendered by the bulldozer, trucks backing to and fro, and months of storage of heavy and cumbersome building materials. It may be worth while to construct strong, obvious fencing (no flimsy sticks and string!) around valuable trees so the entire area around and under the trees is sealed off. Less drastic protection can be accomplished by binding boards or snow-fence sections around the tree trunks. These will prevent gouges in the bark, but of course they will not be of much use if a heavy truck or bulldozer backs up against the tree.

Earth moving and topsoil

Even the city slicker today knows that topsoil is more valuable for future plants — lawns, trees, shrubs, flowers — than the subsoil, which the builder scoops up when he digs the house foundation, or any chance "fill" that he may bring in later from unknown sources. If you are in a position to have any control at this point, insist that he not cart off the good top layer of your soil and that he make separate piles of it and of the subsoil. When the soil is redistributed after the house is completed, the subsoil should be used first, preferably in nonplanting areas like driveways.

At this time, when soil is spread around existing trees, watch that the grade is not raised beyond a few inches. Trees can suffocate when as little as six or seven inches of soil are piled over their root area and around their trunks. When a drastic change in soil level around trees is necessary, as is often the case, a well (really a circular retaining wall of stones or bricks) is constructed around the tree to hold back the new soil.

When the builder supplies the landscaping

Should you consider yourself fortunate because your builder has supplied the landscaping? (By landscaping, I mean that foundation shrubs are in place, a lawn has been planted, driveway and walks are laid, a patio or terrace has been built.) Few contractors today are willing to put much effort or money into quality landscaping. They may go as far as to provide "window dressing" to entice potential buyers inside in

A simple solution for plantings around many houses today is the use of a single low hedge with the introduction of another type of plant as an occasional accent. The hedge can be formal or informal, as is this planting of white evergreen azaleas which is carried right to the entrance and complements the architectural style of the house.

the expectation that interiors will be so pleasing that hardly any notice is given the quality of the shrubs in front of the house, and to the fact that they may soon outgrow their positions and grow above the windows.

The builder's lawn efforts may or may not be an asset. If he has laid sod of good quality (today many contractors are resorting to the practice of laying grass in sod which gives an instant, attractive lawn, thus setting off the house to great advantage), or if he has sown a reasonably good seed mixture, you are ahead in your landscaping and can proceed to other projects. But more likely than not, the builder has planted a cheap seed mixture, largely composed of fast-growing but short-lived grasses, which sooner or later must be replaced.

So the existence of even the minimum of landscaping may not be the blessing it first appears. Often the best solution is to dig up the shrubs which have been stuck haphazardly here and there, and move them to a far corner of the property until such time as they can be evaluated and fitted into their proper niches. (Young and newly planted shrubs are easy to move.) In any case, most landscaping supplied by the builder is only a beginning, and you will want to make many changes and additions to it.

The builder of this house wisely retained the pine trees at the entrance which have a picturesque, rugged form, but then he set out a mixture of evergreens along the foundation which will soon outgrow their site. The buyer of the house would be smart to lift the plants before they become established and replant elsewhere. Ground covers and one or two low-growing evergreens could be the replacement.

Lest I sound as though all builders are villains, this of course is not the case! However, they are in the business of building and selling houses and are not supposed to be landscapers. There *are* concerned builders who are interested in the conservation of the land around their developments and who appreciate the value of native plantings during construction. Such builders may also lay the groundwork for a sound landscaping scheme which will appeal to and assist the future owners of their houses. Unfortunately, the majority of builders, especially those who develop large tracts of land and want to build as many houses as possible in the quickest and cheapest of ways, still operate with a bulldozer mentality, uprooting all trees and leveling every hill and dale.

The immediate problem facing the owners of this new house was the lack of any existing shade trees (as in the before photograph). The house, which is part of a one-acre property, was constructed on a former potato field. Three years later several trees — crab apples at each front end of the property, a white birch, a copper beech and a maple behind the house to shade a terrace — had been set out. Low junipers border the foundation with an occasional taller evergreen used as an accent. These landscaping details, neither expensive nor difficult to maintain, have transformed this barren looking plot into an attractive landscape.

8 *Landscaping and the Small Garden*

Adapting planting ideas to site and climate

When your new home is on an averaged-sized lot (about 100 by 150 feet), and it possesses no special virtues or obstacles, either in grade or elevation, and is generally devoid of any features to be taken advantage of, the logical steps are to proceed with a plan from scratch. Yet, if the house is on a sloping lot or one with several changes in grade, you will want to consider how you can take advantage of such varying terrain. It may still be necessary to use a small bulldozer or another piece of earth-moving equipment to modify or consolidate the slopes, but such changes should be undertaken only for the construction of such attractive landscaping features as retaining walls, steps, a terrace, or a rock garden. Rock gardens are rarely successful unless they are built into an existing slope in the terrain.

What could be more appropriate to this house in southern California — definitely of Spanish architectural inspiration — than a planting of exotic cacti and succulents? These plants thrive in the dry climate of the Southwest and require little attention from the homeowner.

Looking at Your Land 9

If much of the property is wooded, you, as the new owner, may want to consider the advantages of planting shade-tolerant shrubs and ferns before you proceed to chop down most of the trees so you can have a rose garden, or grow marigolds and other annuals, which need as much sunshine as possible. Woodland gardening, in which you can rely on ferns and wild flowers, shrubs like rhododendron, azalea, and mountain-laurel, can be satisfying and, even more important, it involves less time and effort for results achieved than many gardens where maintenance requirements are highly demanding.

At the opposite of woodland gardening might be the home in arid, near-desert situations which can be found near the coasts and in the Southwest. In these regions, the home landscape should be adapted to existing conditions, which can mean growing plants in containers rather than trying to change the native soil. And any plants which are already thriving on the site should be retained.

If your property is more sloping than level and filled with changes in grade, rather than filling and leveling, take advantage of such contours by constructing low retaining walls. Lesser grades can be combined into one or perhaps two walls, but longer, steeper areas may require a series of walls or terraced areas. Where considerable earth moving is required, a small bulldozer and scoop can accomplish wonders in a few hours.

The walls can be built of appropriate stones (of local origin where possible), or the contractor can import suitable stones, railroad ties, bricks, or whatever is available.

Interest in rock gardening is again in evidence, and slopes and even slight grade changes offer the best possibilities for construction of rock gardens. If outcroppings or large rocks are present, your rock gardening has already started. A bulldozer operator or contractor with a truck equipped with a hoist and chain can move and set rocks too heavy for hand labor, although some help and effort with a crowbar will be necessary to settle the stone and see that the grains or surfaces are in the correct position. To look as though they belong to the terrain, stones should be nearly half-buried. An exception would be certain beautiful stones used in formal or Japanese-style gardens as sculpture.

Often one or two huge boulders, which were unearthed at the time of construction of your house, can remain on the property and need be embellished only with a small tree or evergreen to make a landscape feature.

While there is usually some kind of plant to cover every kind of problem area, occasionally the best solution is to forego any plantings and substitute gravel, flagstone, or other materials suggested for paving

This owner-built stone wall serves two functions: it retains the soil bordering the sunken terrace and becomes a rock garden for appropriate plants such as the graceful santolina (center). The terrace itself has been paved with bricks which are an attractive contrast to the irregular field stones of the wall.

patios. The problem area can thus become another outdoor living room. While gravel can be useful and attractive in many situations, it can bring its own problems which you should be aware of. First of all, it can't be resisted by small children who soon discover what fun it is to fling it about by fistfuls! It is so light that it is easily kicked or washed out of place, and in snowy or wet weather tends to stick to shoe bottoms.

Edging of aluminum or lengths of wood which barely protrude above the gravel bed will help contain it and prevent it from washing or straying into surrounding areas.

Outdoor housekeeping: the problems of upkeep

Along with whatever kind of landscaping you decide upon must go thoughts of its upkeep and the time and effort you and your family want to spend on upkeep. There is nothing more personally demoralizing or generally depressing to a neighborhood community than a run-down lawn, weed-choked shrub grouping, or wilting flower garden in which each plant seems to be begging for a drink of water! Certainly no one ever intends that such a sad state of neglect should occur, but in the springtime when rainfall is overly plentiful, when weed growth is nonexistent, and even the most starved lawn looks freshly green, the problem of later maintenance seems remote. However, the very abundance of rain in the spring promotes lush weed growth later. In fact, many weeds are rarely daunted by drought anyway. (Crabgrass is an example of an unwanted plant that flourishes in hot, dry weather.)

Even when budgets permit the hiring of outside labor to take over lawn and garden maintenance, there is a shortage of such helpers in many communities. While services providing for lawn care and mowing as well as spring and fall cleanup exist in many suburban areas, the skills of the men are limited and do not usually extend into the more specialized care of flower borders and rose gardens.

So, much of the actual maintenance of properties must be carried out by the owner. New homeowners often forget, too, that their brand-new home remains new for only a short time. Like the new automobile, houses, both inside and out, soon require painting and upkeep, all chores which vie for attention with the needs of the garden.

Fortunately, there are labor- and timesaving methods to follow in your landscape scheme. One is choosing minimum-upkeep plants like ground covers for both shady and sunny areas of your property. They never need mowing and many kinds carpet the ground so tightly that weed growth has trouble in gaining a start. Other low-upkeep plants are the day-lily for partial shade or sun, and the hosta for shade. The hybrid tea rose, beautiful though it is, is an example of a plant which needs regular attention. Mulches and mulching — often the butt of jokes at cocktail parties — suppress weeds and at the same time reduce the need

12 Landscaping and the Small Garden

for frequent watering during drought. The use of gravel or any type of paving such as cement, closely set flagstone, bricks, or slate, is often more sensible than trying to maintain a lawn in areas of heavy traffic. Such paved areas can then become extensions of a terrace and can be dressed up by the addition of decorative pots or containers for flowering plants.

I have a friend who moved into a new home on a near-acre of property. The first spring, both she and her husband discovered that they possessed "green thumbs" as well as unlimited enthusiasm and energy for garden creativity. A small rose garden, a narrow border of dwarf French

In lieu of lawn and shrubs that would require considerable upkeep, this sloping front yard has no-maintenance pebble beds and low-maintenance ground covers. Ivy surrounds steps built from precast, pebble-surfaced concrete slabs. Pines and junipers give year-long greenery. Rocks and Japanese stone lantern add oriental accents.

marigolds and ageratum, and an ambitious vegetable garden were among the projects started that first spring. All went well until the last few weeks of July, when the entire family left for a vacation at a distant resort. Most of the roses lost all their foliage from a disease called black spot, because no one was there to spray or dust the plants; the ageratum plants succumbed from lack of water. Even sadder was the waste and end to most of the vegetable garden. Bush beans, corn, squash, and cucumbers, which had just started to bear as the family departed, were far past their prime when the vacation ended. (One happy note: they were able to harvest some tomatoes, as most tomato plants reach peak ripening in late summer and the plants survive creditably enough during drought and when weed-choked.)

The moral is not to eliminate the pleasures of gardening because of vacations, but rather to plan gardens around vacation periods. If midsummer vacations, which last beyond a week (most kinds of plants can take care of themselves for ten days or so), are a yearly happening, the sensible procedure is to keep summer gardening at a minimum. Instead, concentrate on spring gardening, a most rewarding aim, as spring gardens full of daffodils, tulips, bleeding-heart, azalea, and forsythia can be the loveliest of the year. Or, in planning a vegetable garden, avoid short-term crops like bush beans or cucumbers, which quickly stop bearing if their fruits are not regularly harvested. Such advice holds true whether you take extensive summer vacations, or whether you stay at home but spend most of your leisure in such activities as boating or golf. Of course you may discover that gardening is a pleasurable hobby. Then taking care of roses and difficult plants like delphinium is a small effort for the beautiful flowers they produce. Even the painstaking weeding which is associated with a plant collector's rock garden is not the chore to him that it may appear to his neighbor.

The second home

Many families today own two homes. Then planning a minimum-maintenance planting program for the first home is more important than ever, for no one wants to leave and return to a veritable jungle. The use of ground-cover plants in lieu of grass is especially to be recommended, and there should be a preponderance of conifers and shrubs that are attractive all year and require little or no pruning or other attention.

Consultation with the local nurseryman or landscape designer is helpful in planning the landscaping for a home whose owners expect to be away most of the summer.

And what about the landscaping for the second home? Unless it is a beach house perched on sand or a mountain hideaway, some landscaping, however limited, may be in order if only for aesthetic reasons. Here annuals — marigolds, petunia, geranium — can supply an abundance of color in planters on decks or in window boxes. Some plants, like marigold and sweet-alyssum, reach flowering stage quickly from seed, while slower ones, like the petunia, can be purchased locally in the flowering stage. Well-developed tomato plants, which make a fine crop for the summer-long vacation home, can be grown in ground beds or large tubs or planters.

Many owners of summer homes become ardent gardeners, especially when they spend their winters in apartment houses. Their gardening activity can range from vegetable and fruits, especially dwarf apples and peaches, to summer-flowering annuals and perennials and shrubs.

Space for family essentials and interests

When considering the landscaping for your home — year-round or vacation — plan the layout to conform to family requirements.

If your family is a growing one with young children and perhaps more to come, a play area close to the house is a good idea unless you do not mind your children tumbling all over the place, out of your sight and a worry to the neighbors. The sandbox is still a tried-and-true arena of entertainment for young children, and swings and other play equipment can be fitted in nearby. The area can be fenced and be adjacent to a terrace or patio or service section. When the children outgrow the space and its offerings, it can become an extension of outdoor living areas. Some friends of mine, with such an enclosed play yard which was sunny and protected, converted it into a kitchen garden, complete with herbs, a few tomato plants, and other salad components and a coldframe when their children outgrew it.

Fortunately, Monday's wash hanging in the back yard is not nearly as familiar a sight in this appliance-happy era as it once was, but usually some washing must still go outside. You may not mind the view of a clothesline full of flapping garments, but consider your neighbors! They surely would prefer looking at a pretty garden or graceful shrub grouping. And garbage and trash cans and containers for propane gas are

Looking at Your Land   15

also unsightly. They, along with the laundry lines of a circular dryer which can be folded and put away when not in use, should be concentrated in one area, convenient and accessible from inside the house as well as outside for servicemen. Such areas should be screened, either by fencing which is in harmony with the house's architecture and surroundings, or by hedges or mixed shrub groupings.

As families outgrow sandbox and play areas, other interests arise. If you think installation of a swimming pool (preferably a sunken pool,

In this garden at the seashore, railroad ties serve as a retaining wall for a sunken garden in sand dunes. Topsoil, with liberal additions of peat moss, has been brought in to make a suitable growing medium for such plants as snapdragon and the silvery leaved dusty miller and a small patch of lawn. The sunken position of the garden protects it from wind, which can be especially damaging and drying near the sea.

16   Landscaping and the Small Garden

as it is difficult to integrate successfully a raised swimming pool with the landscaping of most small properties) is a future project, keep it in mind when you plan your basic landscaping. There is little sense to setting out expensive shrubs in an area that must eventually be torn up for a pool, house extension, or other major alteration. Of course, not all such eventualities can be envisaged at the beginning, but some consideration of these possibilities should be part of the planning.

Finally, before deciding on the kind of landscape you and your family desire, make a list of all the possible interests and necessities you want to include. Of course much depends on available space, the sort of property you own, and the degree of gardening interest you and your family share. Such a check list might include the following:

1. *Outdoor living areas* — terraces, patios (the two words are used interchangeably today), and any area designed specifically for relaxation and entertaining. They can be actual extensions of your living room, but can also be placed anywhere on the property that is aesthetically suitable and practical. On small lots, there is not much opportunity to locate terraces anywhere except in areas adjacent to the house. Experiment with various shapes and proportions on your paper plan. If your lot is narrow and long, rather than wide and short, consider placing a patio at an angle to the house.

2. *Privacy and screening fences and hedges* — for patios, entrances, property corners and boundaries, service areas.

3. *Steps, walks, walls* — of special concern when property has several grade changes.

4. *Open lawn areas* — should they be large, or as little as possible?

5. *Special gardens* — for roses, herbs, vegetables, fruits, and plants which intrigue hobbyists such as dwarf conifers, daffodils.

6. *Greenhouse, home nursery area, coldframe.*

7. *Recreational space* — swimming pool, badminton area, etc.

8. *Service area* — for storage, laundry, fireplace wood, etc.

9. *Tool house and indoor storage* — is the garage large enough to hold both automobiles and other gardening equipment, such as mower, tools?

The matter of passage — walks and paths

In most cases, these areas have been marked by the builder and concrete has been poured. The new owner has no choice but to accept them unless he is willing to go to considerable expense. Yet he can take measures to make them more inviting and less intrusive by special plantings. Concrete step areas, which may lead from the driveway to the front walk, can be softened by such simple plantings as ground covers or a few spreading shrubs such as yews or junipers. A low hedge can be effective along a walk that leads from the driveway to the front entrance.

If you are laying out your own walks, do not make them too narrow. Two people can walk comfortably abreast in a walk which is 3½ to 4 feet wide. If you have any choice, plan all walks and drives a good 4 feet from the walls of the house. Such a distance prevents any actual or illusionary sense of cramped space, and allows reasonable room for ground covers or low shrubs.

If walks are to be of considerable length, should they curve or be laid in a straight line? The answer to this often-asked question depends on the width and depth of your property. A long straight path through the center of a narrow lot serves to emphasize the narrowness. A long curving walk is often more pleasing, but the curves should have some point. Often a definite or even a slight change in grade (a step of one railroad tie may be sufficient) makes a bend or simple curve seem a natural occurrence. Flagstone-paved walks can often meander informally, but achieving this artful treatment with concrete is not easy. Obviously all paths should lead to a destination, and the fewer paths there are on small properties the better.

The edges of newly laid concrete walks can be especially harsh and seem to beg for special planting treatment. A 2-foot strip on each side can be planted with flowering annuals such as sweet-alyssum and petunias; or for permanence select a ground cover such as English ivy or myrtle. An interesting low hedge effect, about 1 foot high, can be made along short walks by bending chicken wire into a tent or inverted "V" shape, fastening it securely to the soil with low stakes, and then planting and training it along the sides so the plants will grow up and over the wire. The rise and thickness of this "hedge" depend on the degree of bend in the wire, and as a certain amount of clipping and training is necessary, this is hardly a low-maintenance project. It is much easier in mild-climate areas where ivy grows lushly during most of the year.

Another point on maintenance: whatever planting — permanent or temporary — is placed along a walk may slow down mowing operations, as it is often much easier to run the mower back and forth across the walk than to be hampered by a planting along the edge.

18   Landscaping and the Small Garden

Putting your plan on paper

Many books on gardening start with the advice to "first make a paper plan." At some stage, such a procedure is sound and helpful, but few new homeowners can make a plan until they have considered most of the points raised above.

A plan can be simple or complicated, made to exact or approximate scale, and on plain or crisscross ruled paper. For some people, the latter is the easiest method, as each square can represent a unit of measurement. Otherwise, use large sheets of paper and select a scale that is not too small, such as ¼ inch to 1 foot. Locate your house, driveway, and walks on the plan, and proceed from there to draw in the proposed terrace and the service and play areas, and continue with other landscape components. Include existing trees, if any, and mark the location of others needed to cast shade on a terrace or to add interest to the front area. Much initial paper planning is approximate, and you will want to refer to the pages ahead for more ideas. Throughout the paper-planning stage, keep the extent of your gardening interests in mind, and the time and energy you will be able to devote to maintenance. You may wish to experiment with detailed planning devices, such as the use of colored construction paper sold in art and crafts stores. You can fold and cut the paper to make dimensional landscape components, such as trees, shrubs, a raised terrace, or whatever.

A few guidelines for basic landscaping

When working on your plan, give consideration to the architecture of your house, the kind of property and its surroundings so that the final effect will be harmonious and not a hodgepodge of loose elements and varying styles. If there is any sort of view or even a short vista, take advantage of it. And when there are existing eyesores, or if you know the vacant lot nearby is about to be built upon, plan the careful locations of such screening devices as fences or hedges or groupings of shrubs to blot them out and to provide future privacy.

If your property is narrow and long, keep the sides comparatively uncluttered to create the illusion of a wider lot than you have. Use shallow rather than wide planting beds. Follow the reverse practice in the case of a wide, short piece of property. Main garden features can be concentrated at the sides rather than at the rear when you want the sense of distance rather than the foreshortened look which actually exists.

Generally keep centers of lawn areas open, although an occasional "island," especially an informal garden of shade-tolerant shrubs between two shade trees, or a colorful planting of annuals can be attractive. The smaller the property, the less "cut up" it should be by unrelated elements. (Such advice is never heeded by diehard gardeners and plant collectors who soon use all available space for favorite projects and plants! But it is good advice, nevertheless.) Avoid fussy, deeply scalloped, or curved gardens which can only add to the maintenance problem and are not pleasing to look at on small properties. Gardens with gracefully and slightly curved or straight edges should be the rule.

Some over-all balance is always pleasing, but this does not mean that every tree must be balanced by another tree, or that every garden bed must have a facing bed. Balance can be achieved with a number of different plants or features, as will become apparent as you work out your paper plan.

If special problems arise, you may call upon your county agent, who is associated with the agricultural extension service of the county. The state agricultural experiment stations of each state issue numerous bulletins and leaflets on regional gardening and landscaping, which can be very helpful when you have moved into a region quite different from the one you left. The United States Department of Agriculture in Washington, D.C., is a third helpful source. To obtain a list of available bulletins, write to the Superintendent of Documents, U. S. Printing Office, Washington, D.C. 20402. (Do not write to the Department of Agriculture.)

What to expect from landscape architects or nurseries

Even if you decide to employ professional help — a landscape architect or designer, or a nursery with landscaping services — you will still want to start off with a rough plan first, since you and your family, not the landscaper or nurseryman, are going to be the day-to-day occupants and users of the property.

And why not employ a landscape architect or designer? There is often good reason to do this. If your budget is elastic, and especially if your property is extensive, with existing problems of grade and terrain, this is a sensible course to follow. It can save you from mistakes in judgment and provide peace of mind. If it is impossible to carry out all the expert's recommendations at first, concentrate on the basic necessities and continue with the remaining components on a year-to-year basis.

In many communities, there are nurseries with excellent landscaping departments. Deal only with responsible concerns and know what you are contracting for before you sign. While you can have your landscaping planned and planted for you, you may decide to let the nursery be responsible only for basic components or for a skeleton landscape, such as driveways and walks, terrace, and key foundation and tree plantings. Then you can add flower beds and other individualistic elements which are reflections of your own personality.

2 Parts of the Landscape

Start with a lawn

A beautiful, velvety-textured lawn is important to your landscaped property in much the way a fine wall-to-wall carpet can be an asset to a room. A lawn's function can be practical in that it is walked upon much of the time and helps suppress dust and prevents mud and loose soil from being carried indoors. Yet its greatest value for most of us is aesthetic: it provides a background for the house and its surroundings and for other features that contribute to the whole landscape.

A thriving lawn with a few key trees and shrubs can be beautiful enough to make up the entire garden. For those who wish as little maintenance as possible, the lawn and a few other plants can be the most satisfactory — and satisfying — solution to the landscape problem. Of course, some lawn upkeep is necessary, but due to progress in lawn research, much of the guesswork and nuisance labor of lawn care has been removed. In fact, there is little excuse today for mangy, struggling lawns. Nor is the possession of a "green thumb" necessary to achieve this beauty in green.

Of course there are people who prefer as little lawn area as possible (they are the ones who make jokes about laying concrete and painting it green!), and all sorts of substitutes — ground-cover plants, gravel, paving — are available for them. Sometimes it takes a spring or summer without grass for new homeowners to discover how much they need it. Some friends of mine, who finally built their dream house, vowed they would have no grass, but after a summer of fighting soil tracked indoors, estimating the cost of gravel and flagstone, and looking at the cool, always restful lawn of their neighbors, they changed their minds. Another couple I know added more and more lawn area because mowing

The owners of this property have greatly reduced the lawn area in the front of the house by adding a flagstone terrace (foreground) and various kinds of low-maintenance ground-cover plants. Creeping thyme fills the spaces between the flagstones, effectively crowding out weeds. Elsewhere such ground covers as ajuga and vinca have been freely planted.

took less time than eliminating the persistent weeds which sprouted all over the place.

Ground covers, which are highly touted as the magic solution for those who want to avoid lawn mowing and maintenance, can offer their own problems when compared to grass. For one thing, few ground-cover plants can be walked upon without suffering damage. Also, many kinds of ground covers — such as pachysandra and myrtle — are leaf and debris catchers, and removing such material from them with a rake is difficult. The effect of ground covers in the landscape picture is quite different from that of grass: grass is like a velvet carpet (or at least should be) whereas the majority of ground covers contribute textural and spatial qualities which can contrast with or complement the surrounding plantings. Both lawn areas and ground covers have their place, and it is up to each homeowner to decide how to use them to his advantage.

What grass requires

If your proposed lawn area is shaded for most of the day, plant a ground cover like English ivy or pachysandra, as the best lawns grow in full sun or in areas of very high or light shade. Well-drained soil is necessary for lawns. (If your home appears to sit on a swamp — and it has been known to happen — you will want to consult with your county agent on procedures to follow in correcting poor drainage.)

Avoid planting grass on steep slopes that may be difficult to mow. Use ground covers instead.

Grass will grow in most kinds of soil except pure sand, but no matter what the soil is like, the key to thriving grass is in one word: fertility. You certainly cannot gauge the fertility of your soil by looking at it, although if other plant growth is present, it may be an indication of your soil's fertility. However, the chances are you are starting with a naked property stripped of all growth, and you have no idea of where your soil came from or what it contains.

You can take a chance and proceed with lawn planting, or you can have your soil tested by a garden center, or send a sample to your state agricultural experiment station. Or if you wish to make your own tests, both simple and fairly complicated testing kits are available at garden centers or through mail-order nurseries. They permit you to test your soil for both its lime and fertilizer needs.

Notes on popular grasses

Local garden centers usually carry several mixtures of grass seeds, all labeled and formulated for various uses and regions. For those who want to know the kinds of grasses that are in the bags, the formula is always found on the container. The cheaper the mixture, the higher will be the percentage of short-lived grasses like rye. These are the mixtures used by most builders who want a green lawn fast and in the cheapest way. However, you need not necessarily plant the most expensive grade of seed mixtures, especially at vacation homes or when your property is extensive. Cheaper mixtures or those formulated for durability rather than fine texture may be adequate in areas where you know there will be heavier traffic than elsewhere.

However, starting a new lawn involves enough effort so that selecting a good mixture makes good sense. Among the grasses you are likely to hear about are Merion and Windsor bluegrass, both quality grasses which will form a luxurious turf you will be proud of, either alone or in combination with other grasses.

Other grasses included in mixtures are the fescues, and the varieties Illahee and Pennlawn are outstanding. An excellent mixture for most northern areas is a combination of Merion bluegrass and Pennlawn fescue. Both Merion and Windsor grasses require heavy feeding and a thorough annual raking to remove dead grass clippings, which tend eventually to smother new growth. Among rye grasses are Italian rye, a short-lived but fast-growing grass, and perennial rye, also short-lived but an adequate lawn for a few years. Around the seashore and in sandy-soil areas, perennial rye makes a fairly acceptable lawn, especially when given spring and fall feedings.

In the South, Bermuda, St. Augustine, zoysia, and Manila are among the lawn grasses recommended. Bermuda grass is grown from seed, but the others are available in plant form as sods or sprigs. There are also zoysia strains recommended for northern lawns, and they are tough and durable. Once the sprigs have grown together — and this may take a few seasons — the result is a solid, drought- and heat-resistant lawn. The only drawback to zoysia grasses in the North is their sensitivity to cold, which makes them quick to become straw-colored in the fall, and slow to show green in the spring. They make excellent turfs for vacation homes where their spring effect is not important, but where a bright spring lawn is important as background for azaleas and daffodils, a zoysia lawn can be disappointing. (A solution to the winter browning of zoysia for northern gardeners who have planted such a lawn, or perhaps inherited one started by previous owners of their property, is the application of a green dye, especially formulated for the purpose. While the green effect which results may not exactly duplicate nature's color, it is satisfactory enough as a temporary improvement. In fact, these lawn dyes are recommended for use on most kinds of grasses, and offer appeal to homeowners in many regions where other lawns, not just those of zoysia, have a seared appearance in winter. Your garden center manager or local nurseryman should be able to supply more information on lawn dyes and can order them for you.)

A caution regarding zoysia: even in the North, the various strains of zoysia, once established, can become galloping monsters, spreading to every inch of ground and enveloping less vigorous plants along the way. I have seen a zoysia lawn creep onto and become rooted in a macadam driveway, and cross a cement sidewalk in its zeal to reach the opposite side. Keeping a zoysia lawn out of nearby shrub and flower gardens can be a problem, which can add to your maintenance woes even as the grass's resistance to drought and heat injury helps to lower the necessity of frequent watering. So ponder the pros and cons of zoysia before planting it, as once you give it a home, it is likely to remain forever!

In the Southwest and in the Los Angeles region, the plant known as dichondra, a relative of the morning-glory, is often used as a grass substitute. Another form of zoysia, mascarene-grass, is also planted. For those who want detailed information on the various lawn plants of their regions, there is no better place to look for guidance than in the special bulletins and publications of the state agricultural experiment stations.

Before purchasing grass seed, space off your future lawn area to find the number of square feet it contains. The grass seed containers will give information on the rate of application of that particular mixture. The amount of seed to be sown over 1,000 square feet can vary from about 1½ pounds of a small seed like Merion bluegrass to 4 to 5 pounds for a large seed like rye.

Soil preparation for seeding

Grass seed germinates best in cool, moist weather, and throughout the North from coast to coast, early fall is the preferred time for sowing. The second best time is spring, the earlier the better. In warm climates, spring or early summer are the recommended times for most of the special grasses for these regions. Most people in the North who sow grass seed in the spring wait until the weather is balmy, but this can be too late. Don't wait for shirt-sleeve weather to sow grass seed!

The results of soil tests can guide you in adding special fertilizer or the needed amount of limestone before seed is planted. However, even without a soil test, you will want to spread one of the all-purpose lawn fertilizers at the rate suggested on the bag. There are many brands and formulations available, but all lawn fertilizers are especially high in nitrogen, the element necessary to promote vigorous leafy growth.

Lawn fertilizers are generally dry materials and can be scattered by hand, but this is time-consuming (except for tiny lawn areas) and carries the risk of uneven distribution. You have probably seen new lawns — and old ones, too — where the grass grew in uneven spurts, some high and too lush, some low and obviously not benefiting from the fertilizer applications. Poor or uneven distribution of plant food can be avoided by using a fertilizer spreader, which has openings you can set according to recommendations on the fertilizer bag. You will probably want to buy your own spreader, but many garden centers rent spreaders as well as other garden equipment.

All applications of fertilizer and limestone should be made after the addition of topsoil, if you decide to add it. Most soils may be reasonably acceptable without your having to add several inches of topsoil, but sandy soils or those quite the opposite, of compact, clayey texture, will benefit from the addition of humusy materials, such as peat moss. Together, the applications of commercial lawn fertilizer and peat moss to average garden soils guarantee that your lawn is on solid footing. Peat moss is a remarkable product, widely available and comparatively reasonable in price for what it contributes and accomplishes for soil. It closes up sandy soils, thus preventing moisture and fertilizer from percolating too rapidly past the roots of plants. It opens up tight, clay soils so air and water can move through more readily. Peat moss can be used in soil improvement throughout your property — in vegetable and flower gardens, and mixed into the planting holes of trees and shrubs. A sensible rate of application for many soils might be four 6-foot bales to 1,000 square feet, but you rarely have to worry about overdoing it.

Mixing peat moss, fertilizer, and limestone with the existing or newly spread topsoil is best done mechanically — by a tiller or tractor with soil-tilling attachments — although small areas can be forked over by hand. You can rent equipment from local centers. When the churned-up soil has been raked over as level as possible, with stones and other debris removed, the seed can be spread.

Planting the seed

Spreading seed in a crisscross pattern can be accomplished efficiently and speedily with a mechanical spreader. Limited areas can be sown by hand, but generally hand sowing is wasteful and difficult for large areas. If you plan to rent a machine, seek out a cyclone type, which most authorities consider more efficient for sowing than the spreader. Avoid a windy day for sowing seed, for obvious reasons; also a wet or rainy day. The ideal time to sow seed is just before a steady yet gentle rain. After sowing, you may want to run an *empty* lawn roller quickly over the ground to press soil and seed into sure contact. Most important, though, after seed sowing is the maintenance of moisture necessary for germination.

A good rotating lawn sprinkler will apply water evenly and gently and yet not wash the soil so the seeds are dislodged. A weed-free mulch (salt or marsh hay or straw, which can often be purchased from local outlets) or a material called erosion netting can be applied to slight grades to prevent erosion of soil and seeds before germination takes place. Mulches are also often applied to all freshly seeded areas, especially in late spring, the least favorable time to start a new lawn. They retain moisture in the soil, prevent wind and sun from drying out the surface, and maintain a low soil temperature. Any mulching material must be applied lightly and should be removed as soon as the grass has evenly sprouted.

Pointers on mowing

Don't forget mowing so that your grass begins to look like a hay field! Grass grows faster during the cool, moist weather of spring and fall, and occasionally you may find that lawns require more frequent cutting than once a week. A general rule is to cut no more than about ½ inch of growth at a time and to maintain the lawn height at about 1½ inches. During the hot, often dry days of summer, the rate of growth slows, and less frequent mowing is required. At this time, it is especially important not to scalp the grass. Crew-cut lawns may look well right after cutting, but such lawns are the first to suffer and turn brown during hot, dry weather. Even frequent sprinkling will not protect the roots from the ravages of hot sunshine.

When you buy a power mower, have the dealer show how you can

28 Landscaping and the Small Garden

adjust the blades for the correct mowing height. Always keep the mower blades razor sharp so the grass is cut cleanly and not torn.

The importance of maintaining fertility

To keep a lawn in tiptop condition so that it is a pleasure to look at and walk upon, a regular feeding schedule is essential. The time to fertilize both new and established lawns is in early spring, when it is generally possible in one operation to apply both a fertilizer and a chemical to control weed-seed germination. A second application of fertilizer is usually recommended for late summer and fall. It is not necessary to apply limestone every year to lawns unless soil tests indicate extreme acidity. In fact, most lawn grasses grow best in slightly acid soil, but it has been found that adding ground limestone, about 50 pounds per 1000 square feet, every few years (not every year) has an over-all beneficial effect on growth, and at the same time satisfies the vernal urge possessed by many homeowners to get out and "lime the lawn."

So whatever else you may or may not do, do not neglect a spring feeding, following the instructions on the bag of fertilizer as to the rate of application.

Crabgrass, an annual weed which used to invade lawns to the complete despair of everyone, can be completely eliminated today by the application of pre-emergent chemical controls (often included with fertilizers). Such chemicals perform the wonder of preventing the crabgrass seeds from germinating.

Renovating an old lawn

If you are unhappy with an established lawn and wish to give it a new face, there are several approaches to follow. One is to mow the existing grass as low as possible, rake to remove cut grass and to scratch the soil, apply fertilizer, and sow seed. This takes little time and many authorities recommend it. Another method — more time-consuming, but worthwhile for the results — is to mow the lawn low, then till the soil, rake to remove pebbles and loose sods, mix in peat moss and fertilizer, and sow seed.

Often only sections of a lawn need renovating. Whether you are involved in a piecemeal operation or are starting from scratch, the best time in the North is late summer or early fall. The second best time is in early spring well before apple-blossom time.

Laying sod for an "instant" lawn

Sod farms are springing up all over the nation, and while the majority of their business still comes from golf courses and industrial and public buildings, they can be a boon to the new homeowner, too. The appeal of obtaining a lushly green, thick turf over your property virtually within hours is undeniable! Usually professionals will do the best job of laying turf, but there is a cost factor here, so you may decide to do the project yourself. The sod is usually available in rolls, rather than squares, and laying it can be as simple as rolling out a carpet. Initial soil preparation is the same as that described for seed sowing, but a level, firm surface is even more important so the sod roots can make contact with the soil. After the sod is laid, it should be rolled and thoroughly watered. Set the mower blades so they leave the cut grass at a height of 2½ inches until the roots are obviously established.

The use of ground covers

Any plant that covers the bare earth is a ground cover, and there are few plants that can match grass in its ability to spread over large areas and be beautiful as well. But grass does not grow well in shade and when established on banks it is difficult to mow. Ground-covering plants other than grass are desirable in the landscape scheme, as they are pleasing to look at and provide pattern and textural interest and contrast. Some, like periwinkle or myrtle and ajuga, have very attractive flowers in spring.

Pachysandra (also known as Japanese spurge), periwinkle, and English ivy are the best-known ground covers for shade, and they have the advantage of being evergreen. English ivy is the least hardy of the three, but there are hardier selections worth trying in the North. In mild climates and in the South, there are many interesting varieties of ivy for use as both ground covers and vines.

Any one of these ground covers is useful in many shaded or even lightly shaded areas around home grounds. Use them along foundations,

Myrtle or periwinkle (Vinca minor) *is an all-purpose ground cover. It is especially suitable for covering the ground where mowing grass should be difficult, as in this space between a fence and cobblestone-edged drive. Once established, myrtle is dense enough to keep out weed growth.*

along walks and drives, in parking strips, under trees or with shrub groupings, on steep or only slightly sloping banks, and as an edging along a terrace or patio. Dramatic effects can be achieved by filling free-form or geometric-shaped beds with these as well as other ground-cover plants. Make the curves of these self-contained gardens generous and sweeping and use one or a few other plants as accents. These "island" gardens can be surrounded by gravel, thus eliminating grass entirely.

Parts of the Landscape 31

There are many other kinds of plants suitable for ground covering in sun and shade. In the most northerly regions, hardy varieties of the spreading junipers and yews are desirable. Many spreading junipers grow no higher than 6 or 8 inches. On sunny slopes as well as flat ground, the low-growing mugho pine, which looks like a large pin cushion, is recommended. Several plants as accents among other lower growing plants make an interesting effect, or plant them by the dozens to make an evergreen, billowing cover.

Suggestions for other perennial ground covers are found in the list on page 32. While few permanent ground covers can be expected to carpet an area completely in one season, by the end of the second or third year they should have grown together. Once such plantings become established, weed growth disappears. An initial planting distance of about 6 to 8 inches is recommended for most ground-cover plants, more for shrubby kinds such as junipers and yews. Before planting, incorporate peat moss into the soil, as soil improvement is impossible once the plants have become established.

This Southwestern house with a brush-covered hillside as backdrop seems to nestle into place with the simplest of plantings. The ivy ground cover gives welcome greenness to the arid setting and needs little maintenance beyond watering, which is regularly done by an underground sprinkler system installed before landscaping.

Temporary ground-cover plants for one-season color

While it makes good sense to plant permanent ground covers which will improve each year and require little later attention, there are times — and places — where you prefer a quick, one-season effect with lots of flower color as well.

You have a choice of scattering the seed in midspring, directly where the plants are to remain all summer, or sowing in rows and transplanting the seedlings. Or you can buy plants, which are well along in development and perhaps even in flower, from garden centers. Naturally, when you grow your own plants from seed, the cost is less.

Among the plants you might choose are sweet-alyssum, a low grower which spreads over the ground, soon forming an even carpet of white, lavender, or rose flowers; dwarf marigold and zinnia; a plant known as creeping-zinnia (*Sanvitalia procumbens*) fine in hot, dry areas; portulaca, nasturtium, and geranium. For partial shade, there are impatiens, lobelia, caladium, and wax begonia.

Ground covers for permanence

BARRENWORT (*Epimedium*) — 6 to 8 inches. Clump-forming and slow-spreading. Beautiful spring flowers; heart-shaped foliage. Shade; rich soil. Lovely along a woodland path or planted en masse under a tree or at shaded end of a terrace.

BEARBERRY (*Arctostaphylos uva-ursi*) — 4 to 6 inches. Prostrate creeper. Shiny evergreen leaves, red berries. Sun or partial shade; acid, sandy soil. Recommended for dunes and seashore areas. Very hardy.

BLUE FESCUE (*Festuca glauca*) — 10 to 12 inches. Clumps of beautiful, blue-green grass for dramatic, contemporary effects. Sun.

BUGLEWEED (*Ajuga*) — 4 to 8 inches. Rosettes of green, purple-tinged, or variegated white, pinkish and green foliage; some are semi-evergreen. Lovely blue, pink, or white flower spikes in spring. Sun or shade. Spreads rapidly in rich, moist soil, more slowly in average soil.

CHRISTMAS FERN (*Polystichum acrostichoides*) — 15 inches. Clump-forming, spreading fern. Evergreen. Rich soil — add peat moss to average soil. Shade.

CROWN-VETCH (*Coronilla varia*) — 1 to 2 feet. Vigorous and spreading. Pink flowers in summer. Recommended for banks to control erosion. Sun. (Not suitable for most small gardens.)

DAY-LILY (*Hemerocallis*) — 2½ to 3 feet. Clump-forming perennials with long ribbons of foliage and handsome yellow, orange, or rust flowers in summer. Excellent for semi-naturalistic effects in sun or part shade.

DEAD-NETTLE (*Lamium*) — About 12 inches. The more common species is *L. maculatum*, with mint-like foliage variegated white and green and purple or white flowers in spring. A second species (*L. galeobdolen*) is called archangel. It has silver and green foliage and makes a more spreading or vine-like growth. Both are considered vigorous but are not difficult to control. Rich soil, partial shade.

ENGLISH IVY (*Hedera*) — 6 to 8 inches. Creeping, vining habit. Evergreen foliage. In the North *H. helix* and its varieties are hardy. In the South and in other mild-climate areas, many kinds of fancy-leaved 'ivies are available. Shade and rich soil.

FIG-MARIGOLD, ICE PLANT (*Mesembryanthemum*) — 6 to 12 inches. Spreading plants with succulent stems and leaves; attractive flowers in many colors. Widely grown on slopes in the Southwest and Southern California. Sun and dry soil.

GOUTWEED (*Aegopodium podagraria variegatum*) — 12 inches. Silver-edged green leaves above fast-spreading clumps. Part sun or full shade; average soil. (This rather old-fashioned plant was once a popular ground cover in cemeteries, which is proof of its durability and adaptability as well as why it is held in such low esteem by most professionals. Useful in areas where the plants will be contained and unable to overgrow more choice plantings.)

GRAPE-HOLLY (*Mahonia repens*) — 12 inches. Shrub; spreads by underground runners. Evergreen, holly-like foliage; yellow flower clusters in spring and black berries. Shade or partial shade.

HEATH (*Erica carnea*) — 6 to 10 inches. Solid, spreading clumps of needle-shaped, soft-textured leaves; very early spring flowers, rose or white. Hardy but may suffer injury during winter unless protected by snow or by a light hay covering. Sun and acid, sandy soil.

HEATHER (*Calluna vulgaris*) — 6 to 24 inches depending on variety. Similar to heath (above), but more subject to winter injury. Shearing the evergreen foliage severely in early spring removes evidence of winter injury and forces new, fresh and compact growth. Heaths and heathers are low-growing evergreen shrubs which make superb ground covers on slopes or flat land. Unfortunately, they do not thrive in all regions, performing most satisfactorily along the East and West coasts in acid, sandy soils improved by the addition of peat moss.

HONEYSUCKLE (*Lonicera japonica*) — 2 feet. Vigorous trailer. Fragrant flowers in summer, but too rampant except for isolated slopes and waste areas. Sun or partial shade.

HOSTA (*Hosta*) — 8 to 15 inches. Clump-forming perennial with variegated and exotic leaf patterns and textures; blue or white (often fragrant) flowers in summer. Shade or partial shade. Rich, moderately moist soil.

JUNIPER (*Juniperus*) — 6 to 36 inches or more, according to variety. Evergreen shrubs with needle foliage. Many excellent kinds for every climate. Sun or light shade.

LILY-OF-THE-VALLEY (*Convallaria majalis*) — 8 inches. Spreading perennial. A favorite of everyone's because of its fragrant, white flowers in spring. Sprinkle rotted manure or rich compost over clumps in early spring. Shade, rich soil.

LILYTURF (*Liriope*) — 8 to 24 inches. Clumps of grassy foliage; spikes of blue flowers in spring. Shade or partial shade, rich soil.

MEMORIAL ROSE (*Rosa wichuraiana*) — 2 feet. A vigorous rose with long runners; showy, pink flowers in early summer. For banks. Sun.

MONDO-GRASS (also called lilyturf) (*Ophiopogon*) — 6 to 9 inches. Grassy foliage clumps or sods similar to *Liriope*. For mild climates only. Partial shade.

PACHISTIMA (*Paxistima canbyi*) — 8 to 12 inches. Evergreen shrublet of tidy habit; slowly spreads by underground stems. Rich soil. Sun or shade.

PACHYSANDRA (*Pachysandra terminalis*) — 8 inches. Rugged, evergreen, and spreading. Dense shade to full sun, but needs rich soil for best and fastest growth.

PERIWINKLE (*or myrtle*) (*Vinca minor*) — 6 inches. Trailing plants with glossy evergreen foliage; blue flowers in spring. Shade and rich soil. (In the South, the similar *V. major* is a better selection.)

PHLOX (*Phlox stolonifera, P. subulata*) — 4 to 6 inches for *P. stolonifera;* 3 to 5 inches for *P. subulata,* which is known as the moss pink. The first, a trailing perennial whose stems root as they touch the soil, has oval leaves, large rose-colored flowers in early spring. Partial shade. Moss pink has prickly foliage mats and large flowers, white, pink, rose, lilac, covering the foliage like a sheet in spring. Sun or partial shade.

PLUMBAGO (*Ceratostigma plumbaginoides*) — 6 to 10 inches. Mat-forming perennial. Glossy leaves turn bronze in fall. Beautiful, true-blue flowers in late summer and fall. Sun or light shade.

POLYGONUM (*or dwarf fleecevine*) (*Polygonum reynoutria*) — 12 inches. Vigorous, spreading plant; glossy foliage and pink-red flower heads in late summer. For sun and dry soil. Very hardy.

ST. JOHNSWORT (*Hypericum*) — 9 to 12 inches. Several kinds, some with evergreen foliage and of varying hardiness. All have buttercup-like, showy flowers in summer. Sun or partial shade.

SEDUM (*or stonecrop*) (*Sedum*) — 2 to 6 inches according to kind. Creeping plants quick to form mats or sheets. Succulent foliage, often evergreen or assuming reddish tints in fall; showy flowers, yellow, white, rose, red. Sun and dry-to-average soil.

THYME (*Thymus serpyllum*) — 1 to 3 inches. Creeping, semi-woody plant. Aromatic foliage; rosy-purple flowers in summer. Fine subject for planting among stepping-stones. One of the few ground covers, outside of grass, which can be trod upon daily. Sun, well-drained, average soil.

36 Landscaping and the Small Garden

WINTERCREEPER (*Euonymus fortunei*) — 9 to 24 inches. Vine-like, fairly fast-spreading woody plants. Shiny, evergreen leaves, variegated in some varieties. Sun or shade.

YEW (*or ground-hemlock*) (*Taxus canadensis*) — 3 feet. Prostrate evergreen. Very hardy. Shade.

Small trees for small properties

The new house sitting nakedly and brashly on a raw property will just not look at home until trees have been planted. Even with the small properties so common today, where there may not be space for more than three or four trees, or even fewer if such potentially large trees as maples and oaks are selected, trees are necessary to partially frame and unite the house to its site, to cast some shade during summer, and to contribute beauty.

The selection of trees is a personal matter, and while it is one of the first planting projects for the homeowner, it should be done with consideration. Catalogues of mail-order nurseries can be helpful, as can recommendations in bulletins from state agricultural experiment stations. Here are a few guidelines to observe as you choose trees for your property:

1. About five small trees (flowering dogwood, white birch, and hawthorn are examples) will be the limit for a 50 by 100-foot property. Or two large trees, such as oak, sugar maple, or linden, and two small trees.

2. Decide what kind of shade you need: high shade for the roof of the house, or lower shade for a terrace and living room, or both. If you want high, midday shade, choose a tall tree that can provide it. Dogwoods and flowering crabs are examples of small trees to shade a terrace area.

3. Don't plant wide-spreading trees too close to the house. Allow a distance of about 15 to 16 feet from the foundation. About 5 to 9 feet is a sufficient distance for very small trees or for those of narrow or columnar growth.

4. If your property is not too cramped and you haven't a shred of tree growth in existence although you dream of woodlands, start a miniature forest in a corner or wherever you are not likely to interfere with other planned plantings or create a problem for your neighbors. Plant seedling birch, dogwood, and perhaps a coniferous evergreen or

two (consult your local nurserymen for good buys in your region for this project) and plant them close together, from 5 to 8 feet apart, in an irregular pattern. The idea is to let them grow together as they might in nature rather than trying to achieve perfect specimens. Later you can trim off lower branches and thin the growth as necessary. Depending on space, you can plant from six to a dozen or so trees.

5. While most upright coniferous evergreens are too large for the property of very limited size, one or two should be considered, even if they must be crowded. In cold climates, they enliven the winter landscape and help set off the framework of deciduous (leaf-losing) trees. The hemlock, although not of modest size eventually, can be sheared yearly (shear new soft growth in summer) to maintain compactness.

6. The oaks, especially the red, pin, and willow oaks, sugar maples, lindens, and horse chestnuts are all magnificent trees. Where there is space they make superb lawn specimens, and can shade house and outdoor-living areas as well. Check catalogues and your local nursery for columnar and fastigiate forms of these and other familiar trees, which take up less space than the standard forms. More and more of these special-form trees are being offered, and they can be used dramatically in most home gardens. An example of one is the columnar English oak, which may reach 40 feet at maturity but remain 6 feet wide. It is hardy except in the extreme North.

7. When selecting small trees, don't overlook the value of dwarf fruit trees as ornamentals. Some, like many of the cherries, are large enough to supply shade as well as fruit. All are attractive when they flower, and the fruit harvest can be impressive. Many other flowering fruit trees, developed for their beautiful flowers rather than fruits, still bear small fruits which appeal to birds.

The trees in the list which follows are suggestions; many more could be added and are available. Their heights are those reached at maturity, but they can vary according to climate and growing conditions. It may take many years for some of the trees to reach these heights. On the other hand, the new homeowner who is eager to achieve immediate effects — shade and beauty — from his trees may feel discouragement and frustration when he looks at his newly planted trees, nearly naked sticks with perhaps just a tuft of foliage at the top. How soon will such young trees reach a size of any importance in the landscape? Again, as mentioned above, climate, local growing conditions, and care are all factors which influence the annual rate of growth of a tree. But, of course, some

The careful placement of trees near a house can help to cool the inside of the house during the summer as well as provide shade for outdoor living areas. The trees shown here have been well placed to serve both these functions. Notice how the kitchen-service area has been neatly separated from the terrace by stockade fencing sections.

kinds of trees grow faster (up to 2 or more feet a year) than others. Examples of such trees are the following: the various birches, tree-of-heaven, dawn-redwood, Chinese elm, Lombardy poplar, Amur cork-tree, golden-chain tree, golden-rain tree, katsura-tree, honey-locust, willow oak, various willows, white pine, and larch. Naturally, the larger the tree when selected at the nursery, the more immediate will be its impact on the landscape. It is possible to have very large trees transplanted and replanted successfully, but this is usually much too costly for most owners of small properties. Actually, there is much pleasure to be derived from watching a young tree develop from year to year — pleasure that is quite different from the emotions resulting when a nearly mature tree is moved to one's property.

Trees for shade and ornament

AMUR CORK-TREE *(Phellodendron amurense)* — 40 feet. Picturesque tree known for its corky bark.

AMUR MAPLE *(Acer ginnala)* — 20 feet. Small leaves which turn red in the fall. Attractive as a specimen, or can be planted as a hedge in cold regions.

BLACK HAW *(Viburnum prunifolium)* — 10 to 15 feet. Clusters of white flowers followed by dark fruits; scarlet autumn foliage. An example of a large shrub which, through training and age, becomes an excellent small tree for the small property.

CANOE BIRCH *(Betula papyrifera)* — 80 feet or less. Handsome, white-barked birch, also known as paper birch.

CHINESE ELM *(Ulmus parvifolia)* — 30 feet. Amenable, fast-growing tree adaptable to varying conditions. Good autumn foliage color.

COLUMNAR ENGLISH OAK *(Quercus robur fastigiata)* — 40 feet. A handsome tree well suited to locations where space is limited.

DAWN-REDWOOD *(Metasequoia glyptostroboides)* — 90 feet. This deciduous conifer is fast growing, but should take many, many years to reach 90 feet. Needs more lawn space than most trees for smaller properties. It is of special interest because of its discovery in China in 1945. Prior to then it was known only through fossil remains.

DOVE TREE *(Davidia involucrata)* — 40 feet. Beautiful flowering tree. Thrives in Pacific Northwest. Hardy into southern New England and like regions.

EPAULETTE-TREE *(Pterostyrax hispida)* — 35 to 40 feet. Fragrant white flowers in panicles in late spring.

Outdoor living areas and terraces need not always be attached to a house. This oval terrace has been paved with brick and placed under a large tree which supplies the necessary shade and shelter. The circular tree bench repeats the shape of the terrace.

EUROPEAN WHITE BIRCH (*Betula pendula*) — 15 to 60 feet. Often multiple-stemmed with pendulous branch habit. There is a cut-leaf form. An attractive ornamental useful where only light shade is required. There is a fastigiate (tall, slender) form of this birch valuable for limited space.

EVODIA (*Evodia hupehensis*) — 30 or more feet. White flowers in clusters in early summer. Attracts bees, which may be a drawback to some homeowners!

Parts of the Landscape 41

FLOWERING ASH (*Fraxinus ornus*) — 30 to 35 feet. Attractive white flowers in May. Excellent lawn tree.

FLOWERING CHERRY (*Prunus*) — 15 to 30 feet, depending on species and varieties, of which there are many. There are many named forms or varieties of the Japanese flowering cherry famous for beautiful flowers, both single and double, and habit of growth. The Higan cherry *(P. subhirtella)* has a variety *autumnalis,* which has semi-double flowers in spring and again in fall. The flowering cherry 'Hally Jolivette' is a small, very compact tree, only 15 feet tall, with double white flowers in early spring. Its size suits it to small gardens and it is a fine decoration for a terrace.

FLOWERING CRABAPPLE (*Malus*) — 8 to 40 feet. Many, many kinds, most being superb landscape subjects. Shapes and sizes of various flowering crabapples differ. Study catalogue descriptions and try to view plants in flower before choosing. A few superior hybrids include 'Dorothea', which has deep pink flowers and yellow fruits; 'Katherine', which has pink flower buds, then white flowers of lovely fragrance, followed by yellow-red fruits; 'Red Jade', about 15 feet tall and distinguished by weeping branches well covered with red fruits in fall.

FLOWERING DOGWOOD (*Cornus florida*) — 30 feet. The ideal landscaping tree — valued for its white flowers, distinct horizontal branching habit, and autumn foliage color. Larger but similar is *C. nuttallii* of the Pacific Northwest.

FRANKLINIA (*Franklinia alatamaha*) — 20 feet. Slow growing; shrub-like in habit in North. Beautiful white flowers in fall. Foliage turns orange-red in fall. Performs its best where winters are fairly mild.

FRINGE-TREE (*Chionanthus virginicus*) — 20 feet. Slow growing, often shrubby in habit. Drooping panicles of long-petalled white flowers in late spring which are fragrant. They are distinctive and unusual.

GOLDEN-CHAIN TREE (*Laburnum watereri*) — 15 to 20 feet. Beautiful small tree with chains of yellow flowers in spring.

GOLDEN-RAIN TREE (*Koelreuteria paniculata*) — 30 feet. Summer flowers.

GRAY BIRCH (*Betula populifolia*) — 20 feet. Common native tree, usually with multiple stems, native over much of the Northeast. Not especially

A flowering dogwood has been trained in espalier fashion to make attractive tracery against the house wall. Dogwoods are amenable to many forms of training to suit the site and to restrain their growth. Pruning should be done in late spring. The Japanese holly, here used as a low, formal hedge on each side of the dogwood, is an equally versatile shrub.

long-lived, but attractive when the birch-leaf miner, which disfigures foliage in summer, is controlled. Apply a systemic insecticide in spring according to directions.

HAWTHORN (*Crataegus*) — 10 to 30 feet, depending on species and varieties. Many kinds, all valued for their spring flower display and handsome autumn fruits. Some hawthorns have good foliage coloring in fall, too.

HOLLY (*Ilex opaca* and *I. aquifolium*) — Both the American and English hollies are superb evergreens, sometimes remaining more shrub in form than tree. English holly is less hardy. Many forms of both are available.

HONEY-LOCUST (*Gleditsia triacanthos inermis*) — 70 feet. Fast-growing shade trees for lawns, available in several forms, such as 'Moraine' locust and 'Sunburst' locust.

HOP-TREE (*Ptelea trifoliata*) — 10 to 20 feet. Small tree, often shrubby. Birds are attracted to its seeds.

JACARANDA (*Jacaranda acutifolia*) — 50 feet. A beautiful flowering tree for mild climates. Not hardy in the North.

JAPANESE MAPLE (*Acer palmatum*) — 5 to 20 feet. A fine ornamental which exists in many forms. Choice landscaping subject.

JAPANESE SNOWBELL (*Styrax japonica*) — 15 to 20 feet. Outstanding small tree, often quite shrubby. Clusters of bell-shaped flowers in late spring which are fragrant.

KATSURA-TREE (*Cercidiphyllum japonicum*) — 30 to 50 feet. Very slow growing. Graceful form and foliage. Often has multiple trunks. Yellow and red foliage color in fall.

KOUSA DOGWOOD (*Cornus kousa*) — 20 feet. Also known as Chinese dogwood. Often shrub-like. Flowers later than *C. florida,* and its flower bracts are pointed rather than rounded. Foliage turns red in autumn.

MOUNTAIN-ASH (*Sorbus aucuparia*) — 35 feet. The European mountain-ash is especially attractive, but other mountain-ash species are fine lawn subjects, too. All have flower clusters in spring with bright orange, red, or yellow berries in fall.

ORCHID-TREE (*Bauhinia variegata*) — 25 feet. Pretty lavender flowers. Not hardy in North but suitable for southern Florida and similar regions.

PAGODA DOGWOOD (*Cornus alternifolia*) — 15 feet. Often shrubby, but when trained to single trunk makes attractive, small round-headed tree. Shade-tolerant. Flowers not as showy as those of above species as they lack the prominent white bracts. The giant dogwood, *C. controversa,* is similar.

44   Landscaping and the Small Garden

PAPERBARK MAPLE (*Acer griseum*) — 30 feet. Small maple outstanding for peeling bark which reveals mahogany-colored inner bark. Foliage turns crimson in fall.

PARROTIA (*Parrotia persica*) — 40 feet. Very slow growing, neat tree which retains shrub proportions for many years. Foliage turns to yellow or red in fall.

REDBUD (*Cercis canadensis*) — 35 feet. Small rose-colored flowers in early May. There is a white-flowered form. Loose, shrub-like habit.

ROYAL POINCIANA (*Delonix regia*) — 40 feet. Beautiful flowering tree for southern Florida and similar climates. Scarlet and yellow flowers.

SAUCER MAGNOLIA (*Magnolia soulangeana*) — 15 feet. Wide-spreading tree with beautiful spring flowers, cups of white to purple, fragrant. Flowers are produced while tree is young. Gray bark is attractive. Fine for larger city gardens. A good lawn tree.

SHADBUSH, SHADBLOW, SERVICEBERRY (*Amelanchier laevis*) — 15 to 40 feet. Often shrub-like or with multiple stems. Slight yet graceful native tree with very early flowers before foliage unfurls. Gray bark, attractive in winter. Suitable as specimens in open or under larger trees in woodlands. Fall color of foliage can be attractive in yellow to orange-red tints. *A. canadensis* is similar.

SILK-TREE (*Albizzia julibrissin rosea*) — 25 to 30 feet. Summer-flowering tree (fluffy rose-colored flowers in midsummer) of loose, open habit. Effect in landscape tends to be exotic.

SILVERBELL (*Halesia carolina*) — 30 feet. Large, white bell-shaped flowers in midspring. A slow-growing, shrubby tree, often multistemmed, with attractive striated bark patterns. An excellent small tree to cast light shade near a terrace. Lower branches can be removed to show the bark. Similar is *H. monticola*.

SOURWOOD (*Oxydendrum arboreum*) — 35 or more feet. The summer flowers — drooping panicles of white, individual flowers resembling those of lily-of-the-valley — are especially showy, but the tree is also valued for its brilliant fall foliage. Trees flower when very young. Need acid soil. Fairly slow in growth.

Parts of the Landscape 45

SPINDLE-TREE (*Euonymus europaeus*) — 20 feet. Pink or red fruit in fall.

STAR MAGNOLIA (*Magnolia stellata*) — 12 feet. Choice ornamental well suited to small gardens. White flowers in early spring. Also suitable for city gardens. 'Merrill' (a variety) is a hybrid.

STEWARTIA (*Stewartia koreana and pseudo-camellia*) — 40 feet. Beautiful flowering trees which are slow growing, often shrubby for years. White cup-shaped flowers in early summer. In winter the peeling bark is especially noticeable. Good autumn-foliage color.

STRIPED MAPLE (*Acer pensylvanicum*) — 30 feet. Often shrubby in habit. Handsome. Green branches are marked by white striations in most conspicuous fashion. Suitable for underplanting under larger trees in woodland; or at the edge of a woodland. Also called moosewood.

TREE LILAC (*Syringa amurensis japonica*) — 30 feet. White flowers in early summer. An attractive small tree.

TREE-OF-HEAVEN (*Ailanthus altissima*) — 40 to 50 feet. Rather weedy, eventually tall tree, but of value in cities as it tolerates all their numerous ills. Fast growing. Suitable in tubs for a time in roof and city back-yard gardens. Its winter frame can be picturesque.

VINE MAPLE (*Acer circinatum*) — 25 feet. Slow growing and shrub-like, its frame possessing a fine, sculptural quality. Grows in partial shade. A native of the Pacific Northwest.

WILLOW OAK (*Quercus phellos*) — 50 feet. Slow-growing oak which always intrigues because of its neat foliage — more willow-like than oak in shape. The leaves turn yellow in fall.

YELLOW-HORN (*Xanthoceras sorbifolia*) — 20 feet. Attractive small tree or shrub with white flowers in spring. For shade and moist soil.

YELLOW-WOOD (*Cladrastis lutea*) — 40 feet. Attractive tree with very fragrant white flower panicles in spring. Gray bark which improves as the tree ages.

Shrubs for beauty and low maintenance

Shrubs as a class are generally among the least demanding plants, and can be used in a number of ways. There are kinds for every climate and region and for every situation on all properties. There are shrubs for sun, for shade (some tolerate both), for rich soil, and for lean; some look attractive in combination groupings and borders, while others can stand alone. Many have beautiful flowers and handsome foliage (the rhododendron and camellia are examples); others offer fall and winter effects with fruits and berries. Some bloom in spring, others in summer and fall. The glossy abelia is a shrub that comes near to being ever-blooming, as its pink flowers first appear in late spring and continue into fall.

The ideal low-maintenance landscape can be made a reality by planting a lawn, a few small trees, and a collection of appropriate shrubs. The result can be an all-green garden, punctuated by occasional bursts of color as some shrubs come into bloom. At the same time, the shrubs will be serving various useful functions — as hedges, screens, and barriers, as ornaments for a foundation and entrance, and some as ground covers.

Broad-leaved evergreens

Broad-leaved evergreens are the elite among ornamental shrubs and therefore deserve special attention. Their presence in a landscape of whatever size is refreshing and almost a necessity: they are never out of season.

All of them are suited to a wide range of landscaping purposes. They make superb specimens or accents, fine hedges for all-year privacy and background, and handsome groupings for formal or informal situations. The more compact and low-growing kinds can be used in foundation plantings and similar groupings close to houses and entrances. Especially impressive are broad-leaved evergreens in association with coniferous evergreens, such as pines, and the two groups work together to bring out winter patterns of beauty in the leafless structures of deciduous trees and shrubs that might otherwise remain unnoticed.

While the majority of these shrubs are valued first for their evergreen foliage, most of them possess other attributes which are equally desirable in an ornamental plant.

The camellia, rhododendron, and azalea produce especially beautiful flowers; the Oregon grape-holly *(Mahonia)* is decorative in its foliage as well as in both flowering and fruiting stages; the American and English hollies are known for abundant red berries, which may remain on the plants all winter. And the rather inconspicuous flower clusters of skimmia *(Skimmia japonica)* cannot be overlooked because of their pervasive perfume.

Paths through the author's woodland garden are lined with rhododendrons and other broad-leaved evergreens which thrive under the protective shade cast by oaks and other trees. In the beginning, some of the trees were removed and the low branches of those remaining were cut off. Wild flowers and daffodils were added throughout the woodland garden.

When shade, whether from trees or buildings is a problem, the solution can be a planting of broad-leaved evergreens. As a group, they are not especially prone to disease and pest attacks. Once properly planted, these shrubs have few needs and are the answer for anyone seeking plants with low-maintenance requirements.

Perhaps the common boxwood *(Buxus sempervirens)* is the most elegant of all the broad-leaved evergreen shrubs. It is an exceptionally versatile landscape subject, with no other attributes — and it needs none — except its superb, perennially green foliage and outstanding plant form. Unfortunately, the common box is not always dependably winter-hardy in very northern areas. It thrives in the South and Upper South and in similar climatic areas (visitors from the North can feast their eyes on the marvelous examples of boxwood there), although one is continually surprised at the number of ancient boxwood specimens which can be encountered throughout much of coastal New England.

But there is a dependably hardy boxwood for the North. It is the Korean box *(B. microphylla koreana)*, which has larger leaves and a more open habit of growth than common boxwood. It is slow growing and, after ten years or so, plants may be 2 to 3 feet in height and spread, depending to some extent on growing conditions and the amount of annual shearing that the plants have received.

The Korean box will grow in sun or partial shade and in average soils, including those that are predominantly sandy. It will endure winter temperatures to around -20 degrees F. and rarely shows the injury to foliage so often encountered in common boxwood after a severe winter. As with all kinds of boxwood, Korean boxwood is amazingly drought-resistant.

There are selections of both the common box and Korean box which differ in dwarfness, size of foliage, or winter hardiness. All are un-excelled for many landscaping purposes in the small garden — in foundations, as accents, as hedges, clipped or kept informal. Boxwood is an excellent component for an all-green garden project.

For those whose knowledge of the barberries begins and ends with the Japanese deciduous barberry, there are pleasant surprises among the evergreen barberries. Perhaps the most tolerant and generally useful for northern gardeners is the wintergreen barberry *(Berberis julianae)*, hardy wherever winter temperatures remain above -10 to -5 degrees F. It is an upright, almost stiff shrub that may grow to 5 feet but can be kept more compact by pruning. It has whorls of toothed, spiny leaves nearly 3 inches long. Its clusters of drooping yellow flowers in spring show up well against the bright green foliage.

Other evergreen barberries that are decidedly attractive include the low-growing, mound-forming warty barberry *(B. verruculosa)*, which can be grown in most northern areas if given some winter protection; the three-spine barberry *(B. triacanthophora)* and black barberry *(B. gagnepainii)*, both reliably hardy for regions where winter temperatures do not average below −5 to 5 degrees F. These barberries have no special needs, and thrive in most soils that are well drained and in sun or partial shade.

The camellia, justly renowned for its exquisite flowers which are often so perfect in form as to appear molded out of wax, is essentially an evergreen shrub for the South and mild-winter regions. It is always a thrilling and rewarding experience for Northerners to travel southward in the winter to see these shrubs in full flower. Yet the gardener who cares can grow camellias in more northernly areas — Cape Cod; Long Island, New York; New Jersey; and elsewhere if some protection from winter sun and wind is provided. An especially obnoxious winter will kill flower buds, but the heavy-textured, rich green foliage is surprisingly durable.

There are hundreds of varieties of the common camellia *(Camellia japonica)*. These and the also numerous named varieties of *C. sasanqua* (less tree-like in its growing habit) offer the gardener in favored climates an outstanding shrub, exceptionally beautiful in its flowering season but always an asset in the landscape.

The euonymus, in some of its evergreen varieties, gives gardeners in colder, dry regions an opportunity to enjoy broad-leaved evergreens. 'Sarcoxie' is one such selection and is reputed to be hardy well into central Iowa and regions of similar winter conditions. It grows to about 4 feet, forming a dense shrub completely clothed with dark green, wax-textured leaves. It is one of the most tolerant and easy to grow of all broad-leaved evergreens in sun or partial shade and average well-drained soil. Big-leaf wintercreeper (*Euonymus fortunei* 'Vegetus'), a shrub-like form of the more vine-like or creeping *E. fortunei*, has lustrous evergreen foliage as well as orange-red fruit, which resembles the berries of the wild bittersweet in fall — an added asset.

Less hardy is *E. japonicus*, the Japanese euonymus, a beautiful shrub of neat habit. It is fine for southern and mild-climate gardens and will thrive in regions like Long Island, New York, where winter temperatures rarely fall much below 10 degrees F. There are forms of the Japanese euonymus with attractive variegated foliage, which can be decorative among other evergreen shrubs.

There are many fine examples of broad-leaved evergreens among the hollies. In fact this genus *(Ilex)* offers such a variety of leaf shapes and sizes among hollies that become tree-like (American, English, and others) or remain low and compact shrubs (*I. crenata* 'Helleri' is such an example) that one longs to plan and plant a garden devoted solely to the various types. Again, here are many candidates for the all-green garden.

The Japanese holly *(I. crenata)* and its many forms is considered one of the most versatile evergreens now available for landscaping purposes. It is hardy wherever temperatures do not generally fall below −5 to −10 degrees F., and thrives in sun or partial shade. Average well-drained soils are satisfactory; humus in the form of peat moss can be added to sandy soils at the time of planting. All the forms of the Japanese holly can be pruned or sheared, or permitted to assume natural shapes. They make acceptable substitutes for boxwood in northern gardens, and can be used as low or medium-high hedges. The many low-growing forms are elegant in foundations. Especially good ones include 'Helleri,' 'Convexa,' 'Hetzii.'

The beloved American holly *(I. opaca)* grows naturally over a large part of this country, sometimes in quite barren, acid, sandy soils. This tolerance of varying weather extremes and soil conditions should encourage more home gardeners to plant the American holly. It prefers an acid or slightly acid soil. Incorporate peat moss in the soil at planting time. (A flaw is its susceptibility to a disfiguring leaf-miner, which can be controlled by spraying in the spring.)

The glossy-leaved English holly *(I. aquifolium)* is less hardy than the American holly, but is suitable for areas where average minimum temperatures do not go much below −5 to 5 degrees F. There should be some protection from winter wind. Although young plants of both the American and English hollies resemble shrubs in their growth habits, eventually they may become trees with stout trunks and branches. Both hollies require the presence of a nearby male plant to pollinate the flowers if a display of red berries is to be enjoyed in fall and winter. The American and English holly as well as other kinds are important plants for the winter garden. (See section on Winter Effects on page 143.)

Mahonia or Oregon grape-holly — its blue-black fruit clusters in the fall look like bunches of little grapes and its compound leaflets are somewhat spiny in the manner of American or English hollies — is an ornamental shrub of value on several counts. Instead of remaining green all winter, its leaves assume a bronze or dark red coloring, rather metallic in effect. The bright yellow flowers that are produced in spring in numerous, tight clusters are decidedly attractive. And of interest are the dark blue berries that follow in early summer.

Mahonia aquifolium is the most adaptable species for general planting, although there are several other species suitable only for California and other mild-climate areas. It rarely grows much beyond 3 feet, forming a rather loose, open shrub which spreads by suckers. Plant it in a northern exposure if possible, as the foliage may burn in the winter if not protected from sun and wind. Winter-damaged portions of the plant can be cut off immediately after flowering, or sooner — if you don't mind sacrificing the flowers.

The mountain-laurel *(Kalmia latifolia)* is a favorite shrub with handsome evergreen foliage and beautiful, bountiful clusters of white to pink flowers in late spring. It is native over a wide area of eastern North America and is exceptionally hardy for a broad-leaved evergreen. It is essentially a woodland shrub and eventually may grow to 5 to 8 feet, so it is fine for naturalistic gardens with plenty of space. It should not be used in foundation plantings, as sooner or later it is bound to outgrow its space in spread and height. The mountain-laurel belongs to the heath family and, in common with other family members (rhododendron, for instance), needs an acid soil rich in humus. Peat moss is an ideal improvement for soils that naturally lack humus; equally important are continual mulches of leafmold, rotting oak leaves, pine needles, wood chips, or sawdust.

Colonies of mountain-laurel in full bloom in their native woodlands put on a glorious display. The foothills and mountains from Georgia to Kentucky are especially famous for their rich stands of mountain-laurel, many of which are permanently protected in state and national parks.

One of the most refined of broad-leaved evergreens is andromeda *(Pieris)*, another member of the heath family. Its habit of growth is always graceful, and its glossy evergreen leaves, bronze or reddish when they first open as new growth in the spring, have no "off" season. The white flowers of the Japanese andromeda *(P. japonica)* appear in early spring in drooping panicles and may last for weeks. The mountain andromeda *(P. floribunda)* is similar but has erect flower panicles. Soil requirements for andromeda are the same as for mountain-laurel, and a location out of direct sunshine is preferable.

Although much used in foundation plantings, both andromedas soon outgrow their space. They are better used in mixed shrub borders or groupings, at the periphery of woods and as elegant accents.

Rhododendrons and evergreen azaleas

The most important broad-leaved evergreens are rhododendrons and evergreen azaleas. They are the leading members of the heath family and unexcelled for landscaping use. Most of them have exceptionally beautiful flowers over a long period in spring, but of equal interest are the many differences in foliage characteristics and plant habits. Their needs are essentially the same as those for mountain-laurel: acid, humus-rich soil and a mulch to protect their rather shallow root systems. In general, they should be planted in shade or partial shade, although the low-growing, small-leaved species and varieties that are so suited to rock gardens are perfectly sun-tolerant. There is considerable difference in hardiness among rhododendrons and azaleas, as would be expected of such a diverse plant group with world-wide origins. Generally, rhododendrons will not thrive where winters remain dry and very cold, or where summers are long and intensely hot. (Evergreen azaleas are far more tolerant of summer heat than are rhododendrons, and many kinds thrive in the Deep South.) While the Pacific Northwest and Middle Atlantic Coast are the most favored locales for most rhododendrons, plants are being grown in gardens out of these regions.

The following rhododendron hybrids are especially hardy and should be satisfactory where winter temperatures do not remain long at −10 to −5 degrees F. Many should do well in colder areas in protected parts of the garden.

'Album Novum' (white)
'America' (red)
'Boule de Neige' (white)
'Catawbiense Album' (white)
'Christmas Cheer' (white, early)

'Everestianum' (rose)
'Ignatius Sargent' (rose-red)
'Janet Blair' (pink)
'Nova Zembla' (red)
'P.J.M. Hybrids' (rose, very hardy)

Some varieties less hardy (for Baltimore, Kansas City, Cincinnati, and like regions) — although many of these will grow in colder regions if other conditions are favorable — and of general availability are:

'Belle Heller' (white)
'Blue Peter' (lavender blue)
'County of York' (white)
'Holden' (red)

'Lee's Dark Purple'
'Nodding Bells' (red)
'Pink Twins' (shrimp pink)
'Scintillation' (pink)

Rhododendrons have been planted to make an informal hedge, screening the back lawn from the street. While the aim of creating privacy for the back yard has been attained, the rhododendrons, during their generously prolonged, spring-flowering season, provide a glorious display for passersby as well as the owners. Most plants, properly used, can serve two, three, or even more purposes in a landscape.

There are many offspring of the beautiful native Carolina rhododendron (*Rhododendron carolinianum*) that are very hardy and at the same time are well suited to today's smaller gardens. They have smaller leaves than the average rhododendron, possess a compact habit of growth, taking several years to reach heights of around 5 feet. They include 'Windbeam,' a floriferous hybrid with early white-to-pink flowers; 'Ramapo,' violet-blue flowers on low, mounded plants; and 'Pioneer,' a semi-evergreen hybrid with very early rose-pink flowers.

Other small-leaved hybrids, some of recent introduction, that are especially worthy include: 'Anna Baldsieffen,' a low-growing plant with rose-pink flowers and almost fleshy leaves; 'Dora Amateis,' white; 'Wilsoni,' or 'Laetevirens,' known for its narrow foliage and pleasing habit rather than flowers, which are magenta and small. The species *R. racemosum* is suitable for the large rock garden and seems better able to withstand sun, wind and some drought than most rhododendrons.

Although interest in rhododendrons centers on hybrids, there are many species other than those mentioned above worth planting, especially when space is unlimited. One species that has received recent attention is *R. yakusimanum*, a native of Japan with pink buds and white flowers, interesting foliage, and a compact habit.

Evergreen azaleas contribute quite a different landscape effect from that of rhododendrons. Their branch and twig arrangement is often especially intriguing and is readily apparent because the leaves are usually smaller and less dense than those of the rhododendron. In spring, plants can be a sheet of color and, according to variety, every tint and shade imaginable except true blue! The list of excellent varieties is so extensive that blanket recommendations can hardly be fairly made.

Skimmia japonica is an outstanding evergreen shrub with large, lush foliage, small but very fragrant flowers in spring which are followed (on female plants) by clusters of red berries in fall and winter. It is a handsome shrub for shady situations, remaining about 4 feet or so in height with an equal spread. It is hardy in Long Island and similar regions, although it is usually listed as a subject for southern gardens.

Choosing shrubs can become a hobby of all-year preoccupation. Consult nursery catalogues, visit local nurseries and garden centers, observe the plantings of neighbors and friends, and visit public gardens and parks for ideas. Regional information can be obtained from state agricultural experiment stations. The lists that follow are presented as samples of the various categories into which shrubs fall and are only the beginning of the shrub story.

SHRUBS FOR VERY EARLY SPRING BLOOM

*Camellia (*Camellia japonica*)
Chinese witch-hazel (*Hamamelis mollis*)
Cornelian-cherry (*Cornus mas*)
February daphne (*Daphne mezereum*)
Forsythia (*Forsythia*)
Heath (*Erica carnea*)
Jasmine (*Jasminum nudiflorum*)
'Pioneer' rhododendron
White-forsythia (*Abeliophyllum distichum*)
*Winter daphne (*Daphne odora*)
Winter-hazel (*Corylopsis spicata*)
Winter honeysuckle (*Lonicera fragrantissima*)
*Wintersweet (*Chimonanthus praecox*)

*Not hardy in most northern areas.

LARGE SHRUBS FOR BACKGROUND AND BORDERS

Beauty-bush (*Kolkwitzia amabilis*)
Chinese Redbud (*Cercis chinensis*)
Cotoneaster (*Contoneaster racemiflora*)
Deutzia (*Deutzia scabra*)
Fringe-tree (*Chionanthus virginica*)
Mock-orange (*Philadelphus*)
Red chokeberry (*Aronia arbutifolia*)

Redvein enkianthus (*Enkianthus campanulatus*)
Rhododendron (the larger species and hybrids)
Tartarian honeysuckle (*Lonicera tatarica*)
Viburnum (*Viburnum*)
Weigela (*Weigela*)
Winged euonymus (*Euonymus alatus*)
Witch-alder (*Fothergilla monticola*)

SHRUBS TO GROW IN SHADE

Andromeda (*Pieris*)
Barberry (*Berberis julianae* and others)
Blueberry (*Vaccinium corymbosum*)
*Camellia (*Camellia japonica*)
Drooping leucothoë (*Leucothoë fontanesiana*)
Holly (*Ilex* — most kinds)
Mountain-laurel (*Kalmia latifolia*)
Oakleaf hydrangea (*Hydrangea quercifolia*)
Oregon grape-holly (*Mahonia aquifolium*)

Redvein enkianthus (*Enkianthus campanulatus*)
Rhododendron (*Rhododendron*)
Shadblow (*Amelanchier stolonifera*)
*Skimmia (*Skimmia japonica*)
Summersweet (*Clethra alnifolia*)
*Sweet bay (*Laurus nobilis*)
Viburnum (*Viburnum* — most kinds)
Wintercreeper (*Euonymus fortunei*)
Witch-hazel (*Hamamelis*)
Yew (*Taxus*)

*Not hardy in most northern areas.

SHRUBS WITH FRAGRANT FLOWERS

Butterfly bush (*Buddleia davidii*)
Honeysuckle (*Lonicera* — many kinds)

Strawberry shrub (*Calycanthus floridus*)
Summer spire (*Itea virginica*)

Lilac (*Syringa* — most kinds)
*Mexican-orange (*Choisya ternata*)
Mock-orange (*Philadelphus* — most kinds)
Privet (*Ligustrum*)
Rose (*Rosa* — most shrub kinds)
Summersweet (*Clethra alnifolia*)
(*Viburnum* — many kinds, especially *carlcephalum, carlesii*)
*Winter daphne (*Daphne odora*)
*Wintersweet (*Chimonanthus praecox*)

*Not hardy in North.

SHRUBS FOR MID- TO LATE-SUMMER BLOOM

Billiard spirea (*Spiraea billiardii*)
Butterfly bush (*Buddleia davidii*)
Chaste tree (*Vitex agnus-castus*)
*Crape-myrtle (*Largerstroemia indica*)
Franklin tree (*Franklinia alatamaha*)
Glossy abelia (*Abelia grandiflora*)
Heather (*Calluna vulgaris*)
Hydrangea (*Hydrangea*)
Rose of Sharon (*Hibiscus syriacus*)
Smoketree (*Cotinus coggygria*)
'Summer Glow' Tamarisk (*Tamarix*)
Summersweet (*Clethra alnifolia*)
Swamp azalea (*Rhododendron viscosum*)

*Not hardy in most northern areas.

SHRUBS WITH AUTUMN FOLIAGE COLOR

Blueberry (*Vaccinium corymbosum*)
Burning-bush (*Euonymus alatus*)
Cyrilla (*Cyrilla racemiflora*)
*Heavenly-bamboo (*Nandina domestica*)
Japanese barberry (*Berberis thunbergii*)
Oriental photinia (*Photinia villosa*)
Red chokeberry (*Aronia arbutifolia*)
Redvein enkianthus (*Enkianthus campanulatus*)
Royal azalea (*Rhododendron schlippenbachii*)
Smoketree (*Cotinus coggygria*)
Spicebush (*Lindera benzoin*)
Sumac (*Rhus*)
Viburnum (*Viburnum* — many kinds)

*Not hardy in most northern areas.

SHRUBS WITH EVERGREEN FOLIAGE

Andromeda (*Pieris*)
Barberry (*Berberis julianae* and others)
Boxwood (*Buxus*)
*Camellia (*Camellia*)
*Cherry-laurel (*Prunus laurocerasus*)
Euonymus (*Euonymus fortunei* and others)
Evergreen azalea (*Rhododendron*)
Holly (*Ilex crenata* and others)
Leucothoë (*Leucothoë*)
Mountain-laurel (*Kalmia latifolia*)
Oregon grape-holly (*Mahonia*)
*Privet (*Ligustrum japonicum* and *L. lucidum*)
Rhododendron (*Rhododendron*)
*Skimmia (*Skimmia japonica*)

*Not hardy in most northern areas.

SHRUBS WITH OUTSTANDING BERRY DISPLAYS

Beauty-berry (*Callicarpa dichotoma*)
*Cleyera (*Cleyera japonica*)
Cotoneaster (*Cotoneaster*)
Euonymus (*Euonymus*)
Firethorn (*Pyracantha*)
*Heavenly bamboo (*Nandina domestica*)
Holly (*Ilex*)
Honeysuckle (*Lonicera*)
*Japanese aucuba (*Aucuba japonica*)
Japanese barberry (*Berberis thunbergii*)
Oriental photinia (*Photinia villosa*)
Red chokeberry (*Aronia arbutifolia*)
Sapphireberry (*Symplocos paniculata*)
Sea-buckthorn (*Hippophaë rhamnoides*)
*Skimmia (*Skimmia japonica*)
Snowberry (*Symphoricarpos*)
Viburnum (*Viburnum* — many kinds)

*Not hardy in most northern areas.

Planning for privacy

Even if you are exceptionally gregarious, you will want to provide some sort of privacy screening. You may also want to screen unsightly buildings from view. In either case, you can select from a large group of trees or shrubs, or use fencing or a combination of both.

58 Landscaping and the Small Garden

The salesmen at local lumberyards can assist you in choosing the correct fencing for your requirements, whether you elect to erect prefabricated sections or to build from scratch. A board-on-board fence fits into many suburban properties, and is one of the easiest types for home craftsmen to build. This fence can be useful in enclosing a small service area where trash and garbage containers can be kept out of sight. One side of the fence can be part of the terrace or patio.

Of course not all fences are screens. Split-rail and other open or low fences serve as important and decorative landscape features by separating sections of a property and setting off various kinds of plantings.

This West Coast house was exposed to the street and the entry had little privacy before the vertical-louvered fence on a cinderblock base was built and the plantings added. An evergreen tree shades the charming brick-paved courtyard and the owners' collection of potted orchids. Oversized brick "steppingstones," wood-edged, lead from curbside.

Parts of the Landscape   59

Hedges, especially those of evergreens, make excellent barriers and privacy screens, and can also become handsome backgrounds for other plantings. Their disadvantages over fencing are the time it takes most hedge plants to reach an effective size and the amount of space they eventually take from small properties. If the cost is of no concern, large plants can be set out to give an immediate effect. If the hedge is to be formal, that is, pruned and sheared regularly so that it presents a wall-like appearance, you are adding to your maintenance program. Most formal hedges, especially during the early years, need special training attention. A tried-and-true evergreen for most regions is arborvitae, and it has the advantage of presenting a formal appearance whether it is sheared or allowed to grow naturally. Faster growing and equally popular is privet, which can be a great asset to your property, whether it grows along boundary lines or is used to divide sections of the garden in the same way fencing might be used.

This front-yard courtyard shuts out a view of an ugly patched street and restores privacy and outdoor living space for the owners. The fence is made of stained resawn western cedar boards which have been recessed from the posts to provide a shadow line. The planting bed in the foreground is reserved for flowering plants in season.

Low formal hedges can make trim, elegant touches as borders for terraces, rose or flower gardens, along walks and house foundations, and near entries. Appropriate plants for such miniature and low hedges, only about 18 inches or so in height, include germander (*Teucrium*), a neat little perennial for edging a rose or herb garden; lavender-cotton (*Santolina*), a handsome gray-leaved plant with aromatic foliage; pachistima, a beautiful narrow-leaved evergreen that can be maintained at about 8 inches in sun or shade; dwarf forms of the evergreen boxwood and Japanese holly; and arctic willow and alpine currant, both exceptionally hardy.

An informal hedge, in which the plants are permitted to assume their natural shape with only occasional restrictive pruning, can be satisfactory on large properties. On narrow lots, such hedging may prove too greedy for space unless a careful plant selection is made. On such properties, a formal hedge or even a fence may be more satisfactory. An informal hedge may be of one kind of plant, or it can be a mixture of different kinds, including both deciduous (leaf-losing) and evergreen plants. They can be set in a straight line or "staggered" with some plants brought forward to form bays. The last effect can be pleasing where space is ample. The bays can become small, intimate gardens, containing a few low, spreading shrubs such as evergreen azaleas, spring bulbs such as tulips and daffodils, and later annuals or tuberous begonias for summer color. A neighbor of mine has begun using such bays for wild-flower gardens, as no other suitable space was available.

Hedge plants can be planted in spring or fall. If you buy large specimens which have their roots encased in burlap (nurserymen call such plants "balled and burlapped" or "B and B"), you can set them in the ground at any time when it is not frozen. Adding and mixing a goodly amount of peat moss to the soil in the trench before planting is beneficial, as it will help retain soil moisture during dry periods. A spring feeding with a commercial fertilizer applied at the rate suggested on the container is also recommended.

Planting distances vary. Privet plants can be set about 2 feet apart; hemlock and arborvitae, 3 to 4 feet. Tapering any pruning or shearing toward the top so the base of the plants remains broad permits sun and air to reach the bottoms of the plants, essential for a full, leafy growth right down to the ground.

The following list of suitable hedge plants is only a start. There are many other good ones among trees and shrubs. Consult mail-order catalogues; and your local nurseryman will have suggestions for plants suited to your property and requirements.

The best of the hedge plants

ARBORVITAE (*Thuja occidentalis*) — Evergreen. Very hardy, tall, and fairly fast-growing. Good soil, ample moisture. Sun or light shade. Can be sheared; never cut into old wood. Fine windbreak or screen.

BARBERRY (*Berberis*) — Evergreen and deciduous (leaf-losing) types. Most kinds have thorns and red or black berries. Japanese barberry (*B. thunbergii*) is most common barberry for barrier of medium height. More attractive are evergreen types: *B. stenophylla*, 7 feet, for mild climates; and wintergreen barberry (*B. julianae*), 6 feet, vigorous, hardy.

BOXWOOD (*Buxus*) — Evergreen. Excellent hedging plants for formal and informal effects, low and medium-to-tall heights. Many kinds, not all hardy in the North. Korean boxwood is very hardy. Boxwood is generally slow-growing.

BUCKTHORN (*Rhamnus*) — Vigorous, very hardy. Tall, impenetrable hedging for large properties, country places. Sun or shade.

CHERRY-LAUREL (*Prunus laurocerasus*) — Evergreen. Handsome tall hedge hardy to the upper South, but not reliably hardy in the North.

GLOSSY ABELIA (*Abelia grandiflora*) — Evergreen in South; semi-evergreen in climates similar to New York City's. Medium height (4 to 5 feet), but amenable to lower training. Pretty pink flowers from late spring to late fall.

HEMLOCK (*Tsuga canadensis*) — Evergreen. Beautiful, dense "living wall" effect can be achieved by annual shearing of new (never go into old wood), soft tips. Shade or partial shade or sun if soil is rich and retains moisture. Hemlocks do poorly when exposed to constant winds.

HOLLY (*Ilex*) — Evergreen. Japanese holly (*I. crenata* and many varieties) with nonprickly, small leaves makes excellent hedge of low-to-tall heights, and can be informal or sheared for formality. The prickly-leaved hollies (American and English types) are handsome hedge trees except in the extreme North. Partial shade is best for all kinds.

HONEYSUCKLE (*Lonicera*) — Evergreen or deciduous types for the North as well as mild-climate areas. *L. nitida*, evergreen and not hardy beyond

Washington, D.C., and similar climates, can be sheared to make a medium-to-tall hedge. Honeysuckle berries attract birds to your garden.

MEXICAN-ORANGE (*Choisya ternata*) — Evergreen. Medium-to-tall hedge for mild climates only; not hardy in North. Fragrant white flowers in spring. Prune after flowering to keep in shape.

MOUNTAIN-LAUREL (*Kalmia latifolia*) — Evergreen. Hardy, broad-leaved evergreen with beautiful late-spring flowers. Acid soil, shade, or partial shade.

PITTOSPORUM (*Pittosporum tobira*) — Evergreen. Fine, broad-leaved evergreens, suitable for mild climates only, where they are often used for tall hedging near the seashore. Fragrant flowers.

PRIVET (*Ligustrum*) — The hedge from East to West and North to South in one form or other. All the privets are fast growing, tolerant of varying growing conditions, exposures, and soils, as well as neglect from indifferent homeowners. The most handsome species are for the South and mild climates: they are the evergreen Japanese privet (*L. japonicum*) and the glossy privet (*L. lucidum*), but the California privet, with semi-evergreen foliage, is widely planted through much of the North, as are other privets. Most privets are also appreciated for their fragrant white flower clusters of varying size and effectiveness that appear in early to midsummer. Despite the fact that privets are so commonly planted, there is hardly another plant more suitable for sheared or informal hedges.

ROSE (*Rosa*) — The best roses for informal hedging are the shrub types such as *R. multiflora,* called the "living hedge," and the rugosa rose, a vigorous shrub, hardy and useful in sandy soils and near the seashore. They are all large plants, hardly suitable for narrow lots and limited spaces. For informal, low hedges which bear flowers all summer, plant floribunda roses. Consult catalogues of rose specialists for varieties. Roses need full sun.

RUSSIAN-OLIVE (*Elaeagnus*) — Tall (up to 15 feet) and suitable for dry soil and windswept locations. Useful at seashore. A fine summer screen for large patio areas.

Parts of the Landscape 63

YEW *(Taxus)* — Evergreen. Excellent hardy hedging material. Many kinds for low to tall hedges; informal to formal effects. Fast growing; can be sheared. Sun to partial shade.

Vines and Vine-like Plants

Because most vines tend to grow strictly upward, they would seem to be logical candidates for planting on small properties. However, not all vines remain vertical; some fly out in all directions, while others are

There are many kinds of yews and junipers — among the most useful and versatile of any evergreens to the gardener and landscaper. There is tremendous variation in their ultimate size and shape, as is shown by this entrance screen composed of columnar forms of both evergreens. Equally impressive in their variety are the low-growing and spreading yews and junipers.

This wooden fence separates the parking area, which is in the front of the house, from the terrace and garden, and also shields those areas from the public. Although such a fence requires no decoration, it provides the background and support for climbing roses trained in espalier fashion against it.

content to gobble as much surrounding ground surface as possible. (Wisteria, Virginia-creeper, trumpet-vine, and honeysuckle are examples of rampant vines.) People who have purchased second homes in the country or seashore are often only too familiar with the rampant ways of poison-ivy, an example of another vine which is equally at home climbing trees, clambering over and along stones, or covering the ground.

One of the major uses of vines — to create shade and screens — is no longer so important, since the extensive verandas around houses, and architectural features such as pergolas and arbors which supported the vines, have generally gone out of fashion. And the planting of vines today can be eliminated altogether by the substitution of certain shrubs and even small trees, which through pruning and training can assume vine-like forms against fences, walls, and other supports. Some suitable shrubs for this purpose include forsythia, firethorn, winter jasmine, kerria, and such needle evergreens as yew and juniper. The garden art of espalier, which is the training of fruit trees and other plants into flat vine-like forms, is enjoying a renaissance, largely because of the limited space for plants around both public and private buildings.

However, true vines can be an asset and can contribute special character to the terrace or patio of today. Terraces or sections of terraces can receive overhead shade from vines which are trained along horizontal beams or other supports. Terrace walls can be decorated with vines, or vines can be trained on trellises or other supports to form both privacy and shade screens along the outer fringes of the outdoor-living area.

Wisteria is an example of a vine which, in the right place and properly tended by the homeowner, can accomplish wonders in the landscape scheme. It is certainly one of the most beautiful of flowering vines, but it can quickly grow out-of-bounds on both small and large properties.

Avoid wisteria — unless you are willing to prune it regularly. Most authorities recommend a summer and winter pruning to restrict growth and force proper flowering. Wisteria vines should not be planted at the base of living trees, as the heavy twining stems can weaken and eventually contribute to the death of the tree. Owners of large properties, who are burdened with an ancient dead or dying shade tree that is suitably isolated from buildings and other trees, might avoid the expense of removing the tree and make it the support of a wisteria vine. You may have seen an old tree put to such use on English estates. (Of course, any dead or dying tree that is actually diseased should be cut down and disposed of.)

The tree or shrub form of wisteria offers an acceptable means for gardeners to enjoy the late-spring flower display in more space-restricted areas. However, pruning is still essential to maintain the compact habit of the plant. Such bush forms of wisteria are excellent choices for large pots or tubs, as subjects for a planting pocket on a large terrace, or as lawn accents or the major plant near a large garden pool.

Among hardy vines, the clematis is the most versatile and appropriate flower vine for most small gardens. The flowers, borne in summer or fall, may be bountiful but small, as in the virgin's-bower, or large and totally spectacular, as in most of the named hybrids. The clematis, in its finest forms, is not rampant, and can be confined to a trellis set against a house wall, becoming a colorful decoration for a terrace or patio. The vines are friendly ornaments for lampposts or doorways, and are especially suitable companions for roses. The vines can use the same supports set out for climbing or rambler roses, and do not seem to harm the rose plants when they clamber over them.

A sturdy board fence, erected as a privacy screen, makes an ideal support for a white wisteria vine. Wisteria requires annual pruning and strong supports for its heavy vine growth.

The vines in the list that follows have been selected for their special value for today's gardens. The list is by no means complete, and owners of larger properties may wish to consult books and other sources for additional suggestions.

Vines for modern gardens

BOSTON-IVY (*Parthenocissus tricuspidata*) — A clinging vine. Long a favorite for growing against stone surfaces, but of importance today because of its tolerance of air pollution. Useful for roof gardens and all city gardens. There are varieties with smaller leaves. (The native

Virginia-creeper. (*P. quinquefolia*) is a relative. While not suited to most small properties, it can be attractive on large and more rural properties. Virginia-creeper is most noticeable in early fall when its shiny five-part leaves turn bright red and light up tree trunks, fences, and stone walls. 'Lowii' and 'Veitchii' are varieties of Boston-ivy with smaller leaves.

CLEMATIS (*Clematis*) — Twining vines of many species and named hybrids, most of them hardy in the North. Consult catalogues for descriptions and follow growing and pruning instructions sent by the nursery. (See comments above.)

CLIMBING HYDRANGEA (*Hydrangea anomala petiolaris*) — Clinging vine with handsome flowers in early summer. Suitable for growing against a chimney or brick or stone wall, or up a large tree. Thrives in partial shade. Although considered a vigorous, far-reaching vine, it can be kept within bounds by annual pruning.

CLIMBING ROSE (*Rosa*) — Both climbing and rambler roses "lean" against their supports rather than entwining themselves or holding on with discs or rootlets as do true vines. They are easily trained and tied to fences and trellises or can be allowed to ramble over steep banks. They require the same care as do bush roses — pruning, protection from diseases and pests, and annual fertilizer applications.

ENGLISH IVY (*Hedera helix*) — Evergreen clinging vines. English ivy as well as other species, which are not hardy in the North, are handsome foliage plants, useful as vines or ground covers. There are many named forms of English ivy, some with variegated foliage. As with the winter-creeper, English ivy can be grown against tree trunks, but should not be permitted to cling to wooden houses, especially shingled walls. The plants cannot harm stone or masonry walls though.

FIVELEAF AKEBIA (*Akebia quinata*) — A twining vine. Refined foliage, its flowers and fruits interesting rather than spectacular. Eventually vigorous in growth but easily controlled. The purple flower clusters appear in spring.

HALL'S HONEYSUCKLE (*Lonicera japonica* 'Halliana') — A twining vine. Rampant, yes, but the appeal of its white and yellow sweet-scented flowers, and its fast-growing habit and rugged constitution under a variety

68   Landscaping and the Small Garden

of conditions make it an important vine. In sun or shade, it will rapidly cover a steep bank, or can be trained to cover upright supports. It is an excellent vine for clothing a chain-link fence, eventually forming a solid wall of greenery and fragrant flowers. Some training assistance at first will be necessary and later the vines must be sheared and pruned (after flowering) like a hedge. There are other climbing honeysuckles, but Hall's honeysuckle remains one of the most popular, and deservedly so.

MORNING-GLORY (*Ipomoea*) — Twining vines, annual or perennial in habit, hardiness usually being determined by the climate. The popular morning-glories of the North are grown from seed and can be trained on a series of strings, wires or slender stakes. The vines grow fast and are splendid subjects wherever temporary vines are needed. Both the flowers and leaves are attractive. Ideal for roof and city gardens.

PASSION-FLOWER (*Passiflora caerulea*) — A vine which clings by tendrils. It bears very pretty blue flowers. Suitable only for the South and other warm-climate gardens.

The blue-flowered morning-glory is a vine easily grown from seeds planted in spring. It is a leafy plant, making an excellent temporary screen so long as it has support. Here it clothes wire fencing which encloses a vegetable garden prone to rabbit and deer attacks. Soaking the tough-coated seeds of morning-glory in water for a day or so before sowing will speed germination.

PERENNIAL SWEET-PEA (*Lathyrus latifolius*) — A hardy relative of the annual sweet-pea which has more showy scented flowers in a wider color selection. The perennial sweet-pea has rose or white flowers in the summer and rather attractive blue-gray foliage and stems. The plants can make a tangle when neglected, but can be useful ground covers over slopes or flat ground, especially at the seashore, as the plants do well in sandy soil. For more restricted areas, the plants can be effective background plants when trained upright. Both the annual and perennial forms climb by tendrils.

SILVER-LACE VINE (*Polygonum aubertii*) — A twining vine. Very vigorous and fast growing, but attractive for its foliage and abundant white flowers in late summer. The vines, planted at intervals along a chain-link fence which encloses swimming pools or properties, will make the fence more bearable to owners and neighbors alike.

WINTERCREEPER (*Euonymus fortunei*) — Evergreen shrubby or clinging plants with handsome foliage, variegated in some varieties, of which there are many. The beautiful fall fruit resembles that of bittersweet. Versatile, useful plants for every garden. Some have exceptionally small, dainty foliage and are slow growing, while the most common form of wintercreeper, *Euonymus fortunei* 'Vegetus', is considered vigorous and fast growing. The wintercreepers make beautiful foliage patterns against any surface, and can be trained to fill confined or more open garden situations. They can be trained against tree trunks, as the discs or rootlets by which the stems cling can do no harm to growing surfaces.

WISTERIA (*Wisteria sinensis* and *W. floribunda*) — Twining vines. The important wisteria vines are the Chinese and Japanese species and their hybrids. Vigorous-growing vines with exceptionally beautiful, usually fragrant flowers in late spring. (See comments on wisteria, p. 65.)

How important are foundation plantings?

The plantings directly adjacent to your house, especially in front and at the sides, are on view every day of the year. Selecting the proper plants may well be the most important part of your home landscaping projects. Fortunately, with the improvement in both design and construction of most suburban homes today, there is no need to smother

70 Landscaping and the Small Garden

foundations with crowded plantings. The problem of the too-high concrete foundation (which probably was responsible for the term "foundation planting" in the first place), while not always absent, is encountered less and less.

Yet some plantings close to the house are still needed if only for aesthetic value. They can mark a front or side entrance and impart the graciousness and inviting warmth we all strive for and hope is present in our homes. Practically, plants set close to the house can still mask architectural or design flaws, even when the foundation may be flush with the ground. The space near foundations is often very protected and gives the plant collector a location for a choice plant being cultivated beyond its normal range.

For the most part, foundation plantings should be executed with restraint, both as to the number of plants used and the number of totally different kinds. The house's architecture and its relation to the sur-

Raised planting beds flanking an entry can be landscaped permanently with shrubs of various heights and habits, as here for a California dwelling; or the beds can be used as a setting for changing displays of flowering plants that follow the seasons.

rounding property should be considered. Always the aim is to achieve grace and final balance so that no section of the planting mars the overall harmony and sets the house askew in its setting.

Some plants are totally unfit for planting along foundations, despite common practice to the contrary. Coniferous evergreens, with a few exceptions, are examples, as most of them end as huge pyramids or cone shapes which soon shoot past windows to the roof. No restrictive pruning can improve them. Unfortunately, these are often the evergreens which, when only a few feet high, are inserted along foundations like hatpins by builders, who then consider that they have "landscaped" their house offering. As suggested earlier, the best handling here is to lift the plants and replant them where they will not be out of place and can expand in growth both outward and upward.

There are a few exceptional places where upright, pyramidal evergreens can be successful in a foundation planting. Sometimes a narrow (fastigiate) evergreen, such as an Irish juniper, can point up the elegance of a doorway; or a group of three pyramidal arborvitae plants can be effective when set out from the corner of a house. A split-level dwelling or one with pillars or columns benefits from columnar evergreens set against the pillars. Houses in the A-frame or chalet style with second-story balconies and decks also can use upright coniferous evergreens to advantage. These houses are now appearing more and more in vacation areas where minimal plantings are desirable. Often a single conifer just off center is the only front decoration an A-frame requires.

Here are some guidelines to help in the planning of plantings near the house:

Keep all plantings low, except for increased height at corners or entrances. Increased height at the corners can mean a tall shrub or small tree planted diagonally to the corner, with three to five shrubs as an underplanting. (An exception, of course, would be a dwelling with windows arranged around the corner.)

Accent doorways and entrances. Balance as well as accent value can be achieved here by repeating the same shrub on each side of the entrance in the case of very formal houses or those of Colonial design, and whenever the entrance is at the center. When entrances are off center, an accent planting is desirable, but repetition is not important.

Rely on ground covers. Ground-cover plants are so versatile and there are so many kinds that often they need only the addition of a few shrubs to constitute the entire planting. They can be set along the house foundation, but can also be extended beyond this area to connect other plantings off the corners of the house, or along walks or drives. Pachysandra is commonly used in this fashion and is attractive when the house facing is of brick. Don't overlook the possibility of having that all-purpose ground cover, grass, grow directly to the foundation.

Select plants with harmonious foliage or flower colors which will not conflict with house material textures or paint colors. Except for every informal houses, which invite "garden" treatment of the doorway, it is generally better to avoid plants with too exotic foliage in the front of the house. Save them for private areas and for shrub borders where they can be complemented by other plants. A doorway garden is often very attractive for houses with recessed entries. Modified farm or cottage-style houses also invite doorway gardens, which can be enclosed with a fence or low hedge.

Keep plantings beneath windows low. A reiteration of the first guideline above, but it bears repeating. If you don't know the ultimate height of a shrub, don't plant it beneath windows it may cover in a couple of years. Often the best way to handle the space directly beneath a picture window or a string of very low windows is to plant a low hedge. It is a simple yet effective solution, especially if evergreen material like boxwood (Korean boxwood is hardiest in the North), yew, or euonymus is selected. In very cold climates, low or spreading junipers can be effective.

More suggestions for front plantings can be found in Chapter 7, *Small Garden Ideas and Plant Combinations.*

The area beyond the picture window

Perhaps the fad for the suburban picture window — placed in the front of the house so it looks across the street to another picture window — is fading. Certainly if you are building a new house and have control over the design, you will place such a large window in the rear or wherever the view through it is more promising than a neighbor's yawning garage. Yet few builders in the past gave much thought to the location of such windows, so houses with picture windows without a view are going to be with us for some time. And for that matter, *any* windows in the front or back or whatever part of the house usually need some living feature beyond the windows — unless you derive enjoyment from watching the antics of your neighbors and their children.

Planting trees or shrubs directly beneath the window is not the solution as far as creating a scene to look at is concerned. But a single tree

Parts of the Landscape 73

of special character and, ideally, all-season interest may be the answer when it is set far enough out from the window area to be framed and not interfere with light and air. The aim is to provide something to look at which will not obstruct the window. Flowering fruit trees, for instance a crabapple, might serve, as there is a flowering period in spring, then a

Sensible yet elegant are the planting and walk arrangements for the front of this modern dwelling. The brick-surfaced walk is practical in its direct approach to the entrance and wide enough to accommodate pedestrians comfortably. The railroad-tie step solves the problem of the slight change in grade; for night safety, its position is illuminated by a low mushroom-type lamp. Low-growing yews form a hedge beneath the windows; spreading yews are accents near the step in the ground-cover area.

74 Landscaping and the Small Garden

fruiting period in fall. During winter months when the trees are leafless, branch outline and structure can offer interest, even though most of the screening value of the tree in full leaf is absent. Other possibilities include weeping willow, weeping cutleaf birch, smoketree, an exotic conifer such as the blue cedar, Japanese maple, the golden-chain tree, hawthorn, or magnolia.

Dooryard and entry gardens

While no one today wants a crowded, overgrown foundation planting, the special designs of some houses — ranch and split level, modified Colonial and farmhouse or starkly modern geometric styles — offer opportunity for flowering or foliage plant gardens near doorways and in recessed entries. Sometimes such garden areas are enclosed by low hedges of yew or boxwood, depending on climate, or by low fences, rail or picket, or stone or brick walls, the materials depending on the style of the house. Usually a variety of plants is used, such as a few shrubs and ground covers, or summer-flowering annuals preceded by spring bulbs. Plants can also be in tubs or raised planters. Often shade-tolerant plants must be used because of overhang from the roof and covered portico areas. Extra watering may be necessary in such situations, as the plants may be cut off from rainfall.

3 Outdoor-Living Areas: the Terrace or Patio

The foundation and other open plantings of your property are important in that they represent your façade to the public. Of personal importance to you and your family is the terrace, a private area, which, depending on the climate, can be used and enjoyed for much of the year, day and night. The terrace has become such an integral component of the home landscape that for many families and especially those with small properties, it is *the* garden. Potted and other container-based plants are displayed; other plants are massed in adjoining beds; trees and shrubs are grown for privacy and shade as well as accent and their special beauty.

Terraces or patios (the terms are used interchangeably today, although to be technically correct, a patio is an outside area enclosed on all sides) afford opportunity for homeowners to indulge in personal gardening interests, such as herb and miniature gardens, bonsai, or water gardening when a pool is added to the area. Gardening here is convenient, as all activities are confined to one area, usually accessible to water and other necessities. It is much easier to install lighting for night enjoyment than in more distant parts of the property.

Most terraces, whether they are in the form of raised decks or paved areas close to or at ground level, are adjacent to the house — quite logical in that they are extensions of indoor living space. During inclement weather, and in winter in northern regions, they can still be appreciated from indoors. (A neighbor of mine always places the family Christmas tree on the terrace where it is attractive during the day but is especially decorative at night with sparkling lights.)

However, there is no rule that a terrace must be attached to the house.

Typical of outdoor living in the West is this fence-enclosed patio. The table converts to a firepit, suitable for barbecues and a source of warmth on a chilly evening, when the top is removed. The fence, made of dark-stained western cedar (1x2s) nailed to fence rails, is a handsome background for evergreens and wooden benches.

The terrain of your property, existing plantings, especially groups of evergreens which provide a protective background, or the existence of one large shade tree around which a patio might be constructed, and other factors may dictate its location elsewhere. And of course, you may decide to have more than one outdoor living area anyway. A small, secluded terrace may become a part of a green garden, a focal point for a formal rose garden, a water garden or swimming pool.

Most patio and terrace projects are within the capabilities of homeowners, but hillside and dune dwellers, for example, are confronted by special terrain problems and must rely on professional help. Major earth-moving operations and complicated construction are projects for landscape contractors.

Outdoor-Living Areas: the Terrace or Patio 77

Shape and size of terraces

In many cases, your builder has predetermined the size and shape of your terrace, and your concern is how to make it private and attractive. If you can plan a terrace from scratch, consider first how your family will use the area. If you do much entertaining and have a large family, you will want a generous area, as extensive as possible for the size of the property. There is nothing more frustrating than a cramped outdoor living room, too limited for both the furnishings and the people who will

Visiting public and botanical gardens is one way to obtain planting and design ideas for home properties. This is one of several patio areas at Bellingrath Gardens, Theodore, Alabama. While the plantings are tropical, the actual design of the patio can be duplicated in any region. The Sabal palms in a northern climate would be replaced by one large tree or smaller multi-stemmed trees such as birches.

As much garden as outdoor living area is this slightly raised deck of Douglas fir. The structure is simple — a large, square pad of 2x4s laid flat over a framework of joists with spaces left between them for rain runoff. Maintenance is kept at a minimum here by the easily swept deck, the plants in containers, the reliance on low-upkeep evergreens, and the ground beds, which are heavily mulched with pebbles to smother weeds and retain soil moisture.

use and enjoy them. If you are faced by a terrace or patio too restricted for you and your family's living style, by all means consider how and where you can enlarge it.

Perhaps the easiest of terraces for do-it-yourselfers is one of rectangular or squarish shape, but semi-circular and free-form or kidney shapes are popular too. Larger terraces are often achieved by making them in L shapes. Whatever style you decide upon, it must appear to be architecturally integrated with your house rather than a tacked-on, awkward afterthought. Before actually starting to work on a terrace, mark its outline with a hose, rope, string, or stakes, and study the proposed site from all angles, including exposure to sun and wind.

Paving for patios or terraces

Here there are a number of varieties and styles of materials, although the surface decided upon must be in harmony with both house and surrounding landscape. In the case of a raised deck, often encountered in split-level, A-frame, or chalet-type houses, the wooden flooring is usually of redwood planks (2×3, 2×4, or 2×6), although redwood is by no means the only wood to use. The salesmen in your local lumber yard can make other suggestions based on your region, requirements, and pocketbook. Wooden planks (or wood rounds or squares) laid directly on earth have a comparatively short life, although squares cut from railroad ties (and of course the railroad ties themselves) possess sufficient permanency for most people.

Very popular now for surfacing ground-level terraces are patio blocks, which can be quickly laid on sand by the most unhandy of home handymen. They are available in various shapes as well as colors and are stocked by most garden centers and lumberyards. Similar to patio blocks are concrete blocks, available in rectangular or round shapes, with both smooth and pebbled surfaces. If you enjoy working with cement, you can make your own blocks or rounds and embellish their surfaces in various ways and with designs, such as a leaf or bird. And of course, concrete is a popular surfacing for terrace areas, either alone or in combination with brick, flagstone, or even gravel. Projects with concrete can be joyous projects for the weekend home mason, but when too much solid concrete is used, the final effect can be overwhelming and unimaginative, no matter how skillfully executed.

Concrete is less heavy in effect when laid in large slabs, which can be separated by gravel, wooden strips, or even grass. Leaving an open square or hole, an "island," in the solid or near solid concrete paving for a tree or other plant combination helps relieve the monotony. Pebble mosaic effects can also help, and give the arts-and-crafts family members a chance to show off their skill along with the family mason. In making pebble mosaic designs, collect flat stones and separate them in tin cans according to size and color. When setting the pebbles — which should be wet — into soft (not syrupy) concrete, plan your design so you can complete it within the time the concrete takes to harden (usually one to two hours).

Leaving some areas open when paving a terrace or outdoor living area permits the owner to enjoy seasonal displays of flowers at close range. These hyacinths, which have been mulched with pine bark, provide cheering spring color and fragrance. After blooms fade, the bulbs can be discarded, and the space filled with such annuals as sweet-alyssum and white petunias, also fragrant.

Flagstone laid in sand or on earth is still one of the most popular and generally satisfying pavements for a terrace, especially when a formal effect is desired. Brick is another popular and attractive paving material. Laying it in concrete can give the family mason another chance to show his skill. Brick can be laid in sand alone, but tends to heave or buckle during winter in northern areas.

It is essential that the surface be as level as possible before any material is laid. A good deal of raking and tamping is necessary before the

Outdoor-Living Areas: the Terrace or Patio 81

sand layer, if there is to be one, is put in place. Then the sand must be firmed to make a solid bed for whatever material is to be the final paving. Various tools are necessary for masonry and bricklaying projects. They include a mason's long level, various kinds of trowels, and possibly a brick hammer and mason's chisel or cold chisel.

Other surfacing materials and methods exist, some of the materials being peculiar to certain regions. If wood chips are abundant in your area, or tanbark is reasonable, or if you have a nearby source of pine needles, which would be appropriate in a small, rustic retreat, such materials can be utilized even though they last for only a few years. Other loose materials — gravel or crushed oyster shells such as are sold for chicken feed — can be used. Various kinds of flat stone are often available locally. Even broken slabs or pieces of concrete can be fitted in loose jigsaw-puzzle fashion to make a serviceable paving, but it is often

Lupines and Siberian iris are favorite perennials of the early summer flower garden. This garden is along one side of a concrete-paved terrace and provides color interest from spring to late summer.

This owner-designed deck, made of Douglas fir, provides level outdoor living space in spite of the sharply sloping lot beyond it. The slope has been terraced by a series of rock walls which have made possible the planting of mixed evergreens and ferns. The problem of fitting the deck's 2x3s to the jagged outline of the lowest rock wall was solved by simply cutting the ends of the boards to follow the wall's curve.

difficult to lay such rough material level. Such small plants as creeping thyme can be planted in the earth spaces between the cement pieces or stones for an attractive as well as aromatic effect.

Shade, screens, and overhead protection

Shade for a section of a terrace or patio can often be most practically and quickly supplied by overhead construction, such as egg-crate or lath structures. For complete or partial overhead protection from both sun and rain, there are canvas awnings and plastic or glass enclosures. "Living" shade can come from large trees adjacent to or encircled by the terrace; or small trees can be planted in the "islands" left within the paved area at the time of construction.

Shrub plantings for privacy, either in the form of hedges or informal groupings, also will cast some shade, as will fences and screens of various materials and designs. If a large shade tree exists within a reasonable distance of your planned terrace, you will certainly want to take advantage of its leafy canopy, even if it means extending the terrace beyond its planned boundaries.

There are many small trees which are fairly fast growing to plant for partial shade and ornament on your terrace. Many can be planted in large tubs to give a further decorative element. Consider flowering dogwood, dwarf flowering peach, flowering crabapple, and other flowering fruit trees, Russian-olive, silk tree or mimosa, white birch, golden-chain tree, and mountain-ash. One of the fascinating aspects of terrace living is observing the ever-changing patterns of light and shadow created both by artificial and by living sources of shade.

Architectural features, decorations, and accessories

Decks high above the ground require railings, and terraces which are not level with the surface also need some sort of barrier or raised edging as well as steps, wide rather than narrow, down to the next level. You do not want to flirt with the disastrous possibility of friends and guests stumbling or falling off your outdoor living room, which can happen when low decks or even only slightly raised terraces are not properly protected at their extremities.

Raised planters, which are also decorative, are a practical edging. They can also be useful in indicating a change in level from one section of the patio to the next. Tubbed plants, usually small trees or shrubs, can be placed at each side of steps. Permanent benches are another way, as are low walls, either of wood or masonry, which should be raised to comfortable sitting height and should not be too narrow.

Other features which can become attractive adjuncts for terrace enjoyment are permanent barbecues and firepits, which can prevent a party from becoming a disaster on a chilly evening, and a sandbox for small children.

Built-in or near-permanent features suggested above should be laid out first; then furniture can be selected and arranged; and finally, the smaller accents and decorative touches can be added.

There has been a tremendous improvement in outdoor-furniture design. The choices among both formal and informal furnishings are as varied as the furniture designed for indoor use. Permanent, elegant furniture is available in weatherproof wrought iron, steel, aluminum, and redwood. For porches, garden rooms, and partially protected areas, there is furniture of rattan and woven willow. You can mix or match, but remember that comfort in relaxed surroundings is one of the main functions of the outdoor living area.

The decorating touches you select to finish your outdoor living area can be as simple or complicated as you desire. You may decide to add a small concrete pool with a fountain effect created by a recirculating pump system; or a simple wok-shaped bowl or ceramic basin, which can serve as a small reflecting pool, a bath for birds, or a sculptural accent, may be sufficient. Outdoor sculpture, along modern or classic lines, is now widely available and can be especially suitable for small city terraces or back-yard gardens. Mobiles and wind chimes, either home crafted or purchased, can be a delight outdoors where they catch even the slightest of breezes.

Large tubs, as mentioned earlier, can be important decorative adjuncts, especially on rooftop terraces, where ground garden beds cannot exist. Really large tubs, those with small trees or shrubs, become permanent fixtures, as they are too heavy to be shifted about (smaller tubs can be placed on wheels), but smaller pots or containers — from 8 to 12 inches in diameter — can be moved about fairly readily. Smaller potted plants can be used too, but remember that the smaller the container, the faster the soil will dry out. This is especially true on city terraces, where daily watering may be essential for the plants' survival during windy, sunny days.

In addition to the usual clay or plastic pots for plants, there are other decorating opportunities to be found in square or rectangular planters, made small enough so that they are not a chore to lift or move. Redwood is the most durable material for such small planters, but any handy wood can be used and will probably last for a few seasons. There has been a renaissance in the use of hanging baskets, once a component of every Victorian conservatory and porch. They can be suspended from brackets attached to a wall, roof, or post, or you can buy plant poles, especially

A piece of pottery serves as sculpture against a combination fence made of cement blocks and grapevine stakes in a southern California garden. Today's small, intimate outdoor living areas offer many possibilities for owners to display crafts and other art features designed for outdoors.

designed with radiating arms like the spokes of an umbrella, to hold an array of hanging pots.

Other plant containers can be found in antique and junk shops. At a country antiques shop, one of my friends found two pig-feeding troughs which she painted black to retard rusting, and then filled with earth. For plants, she selected some small succulents with colored foliage, and then added about ½ inch of white pebbles. The pebbles were attractive to look at, but also prevented soil from washing over the succulents' leaves after watering or during rain.

It is safe to say that almost any kind of plant — tree, shrub, annual, perennial, and most of the plants grown in northern climates indoors as house plants — can be put in containers for outdoor decoration. If you are willing to consider them as transients — occupants of the tubs or pots for one season or so — there is no limit to the kind of material you can choose. However, many of the most suitable plants can be expensive — the camellia is an example — and are worth the effort of being overwintered in cool but frost-free shelters. One of the advantages of container gardening is its versatility. One kind of plant can be grown in a tub for a season, then can be discarded or set out in a permanent garden position in the fall. The following spring, you can select an entirely different type of plant. Seasonal flower gardens in pots can be easily set up; when chrysanthemums appear at your local nursery or garden center toward late summer, a potted chrysanthemum garden can be arranged on patio or terrace, on steps, along or on top of a wall almost instantly. Many home gardeners make a practice of growing a few chrysanthemum plants for just this purpose.

Remember that plants in containers need special attention as to their water requirements. The pots or tubs will need turning occasionally to keep the plants from leaning toward the source of light. Consider the light requirements of the plant. Ferns and other foliage plants will stand only a few hours of summer sunshine. (Most house plants like to spend the summer outdoors and can serve as a decoration when arranged attractively in groups on a terrace.)

Accent plants for pots and tubs

ARBORVITAE (*Thuja*) — Useful accents in large tubs. Hardy. Sun or partial shade.

AVOCADO (*Persea americana*) — A large tree in warm climates, but an interesting foliage plant for pots and tubs in the North. Partial shade. Winter indoors in a cool window or room.

AZALEA (*Rhododendron*) — The evergreen azaleas are more suitable for tubs or pots than the large-leaved rhododendrons. Evergreen azaleas can be kept in containers for several seasons and usually bloom profusely if their soil is kept moist and fertile.

Outdoor-Living Areas: the Terrace or Patio 87

BEAR'S-BREECH (*Acanthus mollis*) — 3 to 4 feet. Handsome foliage plant of classical fame. Sun or part shade. Not hardy in the North.

BLUE LILY-OF-THE-NILE (*Agapanthus africanus*) — Traditional tub plants with iris-like foliage and heads of violet-blue flowers in late summer. Not hardy. Sun or light shade.

BOXWOOD (*Buxus sempervirens*) — Actually, most kinds of boxwood are suitable for containers. Boxwood is a fine subject for topiary or special shaping. Partial shade. Not all kinds are hardy in all northern areas.

CALADIUM (*Caladium candidum*) — 2 to 3 feet. Very showy variegated foliage plants for shade.

CAMELLIA (*Camellia*) — Evergreen shrubs handsome in and out of bloom. Partial shade. Not hardy in most northern areas.

A clump of sky-blue forget-me-not plants in a clay pot makes a temporary terrace decoration in spring. After the plant has finished flowering it can be discarded, and dwarf marigolds or petunias can take its place to provide summer color.

88 Landscaping and the Small Garden

CHRYSANTHEMUM (*Chrysanthemum*) — Excellent subjects for pots.

CITRUS (*Citrus*) — Any orange, lemon, or grapefruit (or any other kind of citrus) makes a handsome tub subject. Easily trained. Not hardy. In the North, winter over in cool window or room.

CRABAPPLE (*Malus*) — Many flowering crabapples will thrive for a few years or more in large tubs, their performance depending to some extent on the variety and the care they receive.

DRACENA (*Cordyline and Dracaena* sp.) — Handsome foliage plants for indoors, but can be used outdoors in partial shade. Not hardy.

DWARF ALBERTA SPRUCE (*Picea glauca* 'Conica') — This marvelous dwarf evergreen grows very slowly, remaining in the 3- to 4-foot range for many years. Sun. Hardy.

ELEPHANT'S-EAR (*Colocasia esculenta*) — 3 to 4 feet. Large, rather course foliage. Useful in shade. Not hardy. Grown from tubers.

FATSIA (*Fatsia japonica*) — Large shrub with large, deeply cut foliage. Handsome foliage plant for shade. Not hardy in North.

FERNS — Wide choice here of both tender and hardy ferns. Shade.

FIRETHORN (*Pyracantha*) — Very versatile shrub and suitable for tubs. Hardy.

FUCHSIA (*Fuchsia*) — Superb pot, tub, or hanging-basket subjects for the terrace or patio. Beautiful, exotic flowers in summer in northern areas; year-round in mild climates. Partial shade.

GARDENIA (*Gardenia jasminoides*) — Attractive evergreen shrubs with fragrant white flowers. Not reliably hardy north of Washington, D.C.

GERANIUM (*Pelargonium*) — Large geranium plants make decorative accents. Smaller plants are standard selections for planters and window boxes. Some of the scented-leaf geraniums can grow into handsome large pot plants which are decorative and pleasantly aromatic.

Outdoor-Living Areas: the Terrace or Patio 89

GOLD-DUST TREE (*Aucuba japonica*) — 4 to 5 feet. Evergreen shrub, its leathery foliage spotted with yellow. Partial shade. Hardy to about 5 degrees F.

GOLDEN-CHAIN TREE (*Laburnum watereri*) — This small tree makes a beautiful tub subject while in bloom. Hardy.

HOLLY (*Ilex*) — All kinds are suitable, so the choice is a wide one.

The pot garden of Dumbarton Oaks in Washington, D.C., in spring. Among the plants in pots and other containers are azalea, camellia, columbine, various kinds of citrus, oleander, and lily. As these plants complete their blooming period, they are replaced by others appropriate to the season.

HYDRANGEA (*Hydrangea macrophylla*) — The "French" hydrangea, with its long-lasting pink or blue flowers (color depends on soil — flowers are blue in acid soil, pink in alkaline) has always been a popular pot or tub plant. Discard or plant in garden after blooms are faded.

JAPANESE MAPLE (*Acer palmatum*) — Excellent subject for tubs. Hardy.

JUNIPER (*Juniperus*) — All kinds.

KAFIR-LILY (*Clivia miniata*) — 2 feet. Traditional pot or tub subjects with iris-like foliage and orange flower heads in early summer.

LANTANA (*Lantana*) — Once important pot subjects, less commonly seen today. Sun. Not hardy.

LEMON-VERBENA (*Lippia citriodora*) — Old-fashioned tub subject with lemon-scented foliage, delightful in partial shade on a terrace.

MARGUERITE DAISY (*Chrysanthemum frutescens*) — Shrubby daisy with yellow or white flowers. Not hardy.

MUGHO PINE (*Pinus mugo*) — There are many forms of this dwarf pine, some being more truly dwarf or slow growing than others. Hardy. Many other kinds of pines, dwarf or standard, can be grown in large containers for several years.

NORFOLK ISLAND-PINE (*Araucaria excelsa*) — Beautiful coniferous evergreen, usually grown as house plant in the North.

OLEANDER (*Nerium oleander*) — These tree-like shrubs are attractive tub subjects. Not hardy. In the North, the plants must spend the winter in a cool, frost-free room.

PRIVET (*Ligustrum*) — All privet species can be potted or tubbed. They are tolerant of summer heat and wind on roof gardens. Most deciduous kinds are hardy, the evergreen kinds less so.

ROSE (*Rosa*) — Hybrid tea and floribunda roses do surprisingly well in tubs. Tubs of tree roses make formal, colorful accents. Sun. Hardy.

This compact city garden features a half-moon pool with a trickle of a fountain serviced by a small pump which recirculates the water. The mood of the garden is mainly refreshing and restful, but touches of color are provided by ivy-leaf geraniums in hanging containers, above the bamboo screen where they receive more direct sunshine, and by rose- and white-flowered sweet-alyssum plants in front of the pool. Plate 1

Gardens in containers offer a satisfying way to decorate a patio or terrace area. Here three concrete bowls have become individual gardens of cactus and succulent plants. Their essential requirement is a fully sunny exposure. Only occasional watering—enough to prevent the plants from shriveling—is necessary.
Plate 2

A mulch of wood chips is attractive to look at and pleasant to walk upon, and it will suppress the growth of weeds. It is comparatively reasonable in price and will last for three or four years. Similar materials, suitable for surfacing woodland paths or informal terrace areas and for mulching around trees and shrubs, are pine bark, tanbark, and pine needles. Plate 3

A miniature pool has been created at the edge of a woodland by sinking a rectangular galvanized washtub in the ground. The placement of rocks around the edge, the spreading blue-flowered ajuga, and sculptural accents in the form of concrete rabbits combine to conceal the origin of the pool. Former bathtubs and other discarded receptacles can be transformed into small garden pools and birdbaths. Plate 4

Sophisticated adaptation of Japanese landscaping principles is shown in this Carmel, California, garden. It is essentially a garden of green plants selected for form and texture rather than color. The formality of the gravel-and-concrete patio area has been lessened by the random yet always artful arrangement of stones used in Japanese fashion to simulate a stream bed. Plate 5

Modern homes of spare architectural detail often require a minimum of planting near their foundations. The simple planting here, which is of the evergreen shrub, yew, and white petunias and geraniums, can be duplicated in any region of the country. Yews are available in dwarf, spreading, or upright forms and can be selected for a number of situations. Plate 6

ROSEMARY (*Rosmarinus officinalis*) — Most of us are more familiar with the rosemary as a small potted plant for a narrow window sill, but this culinary herb is a true shrub which can reach 6 feet or so in its native Mediterranean and similar mild-climate regions. Small potted plants often grow fairly quickly and in a few years make handsome specimens for large terra-cotta pots. (When the plants sulk, it may be an indication that they are lime starved. Apply a little lime or wood ashes from the fireplace and watch the foliage color improve.) Rosemary likes a sunny situation. In the winter the plants need a cool, sunny window and only enough water to prevent wilting.

SPANISH-BAYONET (*Yucca*) — Stiff foliage plants for exotic effects in full sun.

SWEET BAY (*Laurus nobilis*) — The laurel of the Mediterranean makes a handsome tub shrub which can be pruned and trained as desired. Not hardy. The leaves, when dried, are the "bay leaf" of cuisine.

WILLOW (*Salix*) — Many kinds do well in large tubs. Soil must be kept moist. Hardy. Sun or light shade.

YEW (*Taxus*) — Excellent tub evergreens. For elegant accents at entrance, select narrow forms. Hardy. Sun or light shade.

YEW PODOCARPUS (*Podocarpus macrophyllus*) — Popular shrubby house plant in the North. Tubbed plants can be moved to partially shaded terrace or outdoor living-room area for summer.

City terraces, gardens, and window boxes

The pleasures and rewards of gardening in the city — whether in a mere window box or on a terrace or rooftop high above street level — far outnumber the obvious problems and pitfalls, which mostly arise from atmospheric pollution and an almost constant drift of grime and soot. Plants growing in tubs and containers on exposed terraces are often subjected to drying winds during both summer and winter, yet plants in city back yards are often uniquely protected from the elements by surrounding buildings. In fact, city back-yard gardening often does not differ drastically from that of nearby suburbs. Often the entire back-yard

This small city terrace is enclosed by sections of stockade fencing for privacy and protection from strong wind. The owners have wisely selected furniture of open, simple design which does not detract from the garden mood created by the plants. The brick walls of the building are covered by vines while geraniums supply touches of color beneath them.

space is treated as a terrace or patio area surfaced with one kind of — or a combination of — pavings, such as brick, flagstone, or concrete. Paving the entire back yard eliminates the need for grassy areas, which are a nuisance to maintain, especially if shade is extensive and air circulation is poor — two conditions common in many city back yards.

The suggestions concerning fencing made earlier apply especially to city back yards where fences provide both privacy and protection as well as background for plants. The dominating plants are usually

Outdoor-Living Areas: the Terrace or Patio

shrubs and a few accent trees and such ground covers as English ivy, pachysandra, ajuga, or myrtle. Spring bulbs — crocus, daffodils, tulips, and hyacinths — can be satisfactory in front of the shrubs. Later annuals can be set out for summer color, but unless the back yard receives several hours of sunshine, the city gardener will achieve the best effects with foliage plants. While most city gardens offer opportunity for ground beds, plants in containers — pots, tubs, planters, and often boxes at the windows — contribute architectural interest and an authentic patio effect.

The design of city back-yard terraces and gardens can be of balanced formality or studied informality — with the same rules being observed as in more extensive properties. However, because of the limited space occupied by most city gardens, clutter and overplanting should be avoided.

Rooftop gardens and the terraces which exist today on the sides of most new apartment houses are usually very sunny and provide opportunity for growing many flowering plants that will not survive in shaded ground-level city gardens. Florist and garden shops exist in all cities, and in spring and early summer offer a wide array of plant material as well as soil, peat moss, containers, and fencing.

The plants for such gardens can be changed frequently with the seasons. As spring-blooming plants fade, they can be discarded for budded or even flowering specimens for early summer. For fall display, potted chrysanthemums can be selected. Of course, geraniums and such annuals as petunias and marigolds should flower nearly all summer, especially if they are watered as necessary and fertilized several times during the summer. Washing the soot off foliage must be done as frequently as indicated by the accumulations — perhaps weekly in many cities.

Indoor-outdoor carpeting can be very useful in rooftop and other sky gardens. Or if you have a yen for the sight of a cool, refreshing "lawn," you can buy plastic grass mats, which are so authentic in appearance and feel that you think you are walking on actual sod. Sources for these artificial lawns can usually be found in the Yellow Pages of telephone books. Many city garden shops now sell sections of any dimension directly.

Many of the plants mentioned throughout this book will do well in the majority of city and rooftop garden situations, although in the latter, their longevity may be considerably less than in normal ground-bed gardens. Especially durable in cities are tree-of-heaven (*Ailanthus al-*

Details are important in city gardens where limited space and excessive shade may dictate the type of gardening activity. A stone fruit basket makes an appropriate ornament on the low brick wall which also provides space for two potted camellia plants. The camellias, in attractive Italian clay pots which harmonize with the brick wall, must be wintered indoors in a cool window in the North.

tissima), catalpa, maidenhair tree (*Ginkgo biloba*), Russian-olive (*Elaeagnus*), most fruit trees, star magnolia (*Magnolia stellata*), poplar (*Populus*), and the weeping willow — so long as it receives ample moisture. Most shrubs will be satisfactory, including such evergreen types as rhododendron and evergreen azalea (for partial shade) and the Japanese holly (*Ilex crenata*).

Apartment dwellers who do not have access to rooftops, terraces, or back yards often have windows with wide enough ledges for window boxes. Metal, plastic, or wooden boxes can usually be purchased from five-and-tens, department stores, or florist or garden shops. If you can't find boxes that exactly fit the dimensions of your window or windows, you can purchase two or more smaller boxes, or construct your own. The depth of the boxes should be at least 8 inches and there should be small holes for drainage of excessive water. Boxes must be securely fastened to the windows so there will be no chance of a box slipping off and causing havoc below. (Boxes in suburban windows are usually supported by brackets.)

You can buy premixed soil; regular feeding and watering schedules are as necessary with window boxes as with plants growing in any other container or pot. In hot, dry weather, the boxes may need daily watering. Avoid keeping the soil soggy and waterlogged, though.

Annuals are the easiest plants to grow in city window boxes, and can be sown in seed form directly in the boxes, or you can buy young plants at a florist or garden shop. Seeds of the climbing morning-glory vine can be planted at each end of the boxes and trained around the window.

During the winter months, window boxes can remain decorative if you stuff them with cut evergreen branches. Additional decorative effects can result if you insert an occasional artificial flower spray — but with discretion to avoid a garish, unnatural look.

4 Tips for Easier Maintenance

It may take a season or two, or three or four, before you reach maximum efficiency in carrying out the maintenance duties your property requires. Most plantings — from lawns to trees and shrubs — need more care the first few years in the matter of watering and weed-control attention. Along the way you will discover short cuts yourself, which save time you can devote to other activities or to the more pleasurable aspects of gardening. Check the following points — one or all may have meaning in your situation.

Mowing strips

A term much used today, which simply refers to any method of reducing grass growth close to walls, tree trunks, and garden borders out of reach of a lawn mower. To save the labor of hand clipping the grass in such areas, strips about a foot or so wide are paved with cement, brick, flagstone, or gravel. Such strips save time but also prevent nicks and deeper gouges in tree trunks by careless handling of the mower.

A tool house for storage

A separate place for garden equipment and supplies often becomes necessary unless your garage has elastic walls. It can be located closer to the area of most of your gardening activity, and can save the time and

98 Landscaping and the Small Garden

effort of running back and forth for necessary equipment. Be sure it is attractive. Some of the prefabricated aluminum tool houses are too ornate; those of redwood, pine, or other wood can be attractive and fit into the landscape more naturally. Building your own, if you are a home craftsman, may be preferable. Its style should be in some harmony with your house and surroundings. Before buying or building, consider the items you will be storing and the amount of space you are likely to need. Acquiring too small a house hardly solves a problem, and only adds another.

Basic tools

The matter of acquiring the tools to store in the tool house deserves some consideration, as beginners (and even more experienced gardeners) are often tempted beyond their needs by the attractive, glittering displays of new tools in garden centers and hardware stores. Many garden tools are mere gadgets — flashingly designed and presented — but in reality are ill equipped to solve the maintenance problems promised by the manufacturer. Others may be so poorly manufactured in the first place that they fall apart after only a few hours of use.

The kinds and numbers of tools necessary depend on the size of your property, the extent of your gardening interests beyond basic maintenance and initial landscaping efforts, and, to some degree, your proclivity in handling and using tools. Also, certain tools, especially those in the power category, may be required at an early stage in the development of a property's landscaping but later will be unnecessary and just take valuable storage space. A power tiller or tractor — to cultivate the soil for new lawns or new large garden areas — is an example of a tool often of only temporary need. In such a case, renting is the sensible solution, no matter how much you may be tempted to buy. However, another power tool, the electric hedge trimmer (available also in a cordless model), may be of enough steady use to warrant purchase rather than rental. Hedges require from one to two or more trimmings a year, and the lazy homeowner is more likely to follow through on this tedious maintenance if the trimmer is always at hand.

As a start, the new gardener should consider acquiring the following basic tools:

Tips for Easier Maintenance

- wheelbarrow — More than one may be convenient and even necessary for properties between a half acre and acre or larger.
- long-handled shovels — Short-handled shovels or forks can cause shoulder and back strain if used for long periods to dig holes or move earth.
- sharp-bladed spade — For transplanting, especially trees and shrubs.
- garden rake — Of heavy-duty metal, for smoothing lawn and garden surface before seed sowing or setting out plants.
- lawn rake — Lightweight bamboo or metal to remove leaves in the autumn or spring, and to whisk up lawn trimmings not caught in the power mower's grass catcher.
- power mower — Power mowers are a boon and necessity for today's extensive lawn areas. For very small lawn areas, don't rush into buying a power mower. Consider, instead, the old-fashioned hand mower (but one of today's improved lightweight models). It is definitely quieter, and does not demand the care and precautions associated with power equipment.
- grass trimmer — There are short-handled trimmers (the old sheep-shearer principle is still considered by many to be the best). For extensive clipping, such as along a walk, drive, or garden border, there are various kinds of grass trimmers which can be wheeled along by the operator from an erect rather than the more uncomfortable kneeling or bending position necessary with the short-handled shears. Cordless electric models also have been introduced.
- long-handled clippers — For shearing and shaping. The electric hedge trimmers mentioned above are very convenient for shearing young evergreens.
- sundry trowels (wide and narrow bladed), pruners and possibly spray equipment.

Mulches and mulching

Mulches will not reduce garden maintenance to the point where you can live in a hammock or armchair, yet they can be of mighty assistance in the battle of weed control and maintaining soil moisture. The weeds that do penetrate a mulch are much easier to pull than those in un-

100 Landscaping and the Small Garden

mulched ground. Mulches can be attractive, providing a neat, finished appearance as well as change in texture and color to a planting.

The best-appearing mulches are buckwheat hulls, sawdust, shredded pine bark, tanbark, not too coarsely cut wood chips, pine needles, leafmold, and very coarse peat moss of the grade used as poultry bedding. The regular garden grade of peat moss, although attractive in color and texture, is more valuable when added to the soil than when spread as a mulch. If left on the surface it tends to blow away, or it can mat together to form a surface impenetrable to rain or artificially applied water. Less attractive in appearance but functional are straw or hay mulches (be sure they do not contain weed seeds), ground sugar cane, various kinds of seaweed and beach debris, homemade compost (the remains of lawn clippings, leaves, and garbage which have been collected, piled with soil, and allowed to partially decompose).

To be effective, 2 to 3 inches of a mulch should be spread. Materials such as sawdust, ground corncobs, ground sugar cane, and wood chips can deplete the soil of nitrogen as they decay, thus starving the plants in the vicinity. Sprinkling a commercial fertilizer high in nitrogen over the area to replenish the nitrogen is recommended for a few times during the growing season.

Underground sprinkling system

The installation of a sprinkling system can save a good deal of time and energy spent fussing with and moving hoses and sprinklers during dry weather, especially if your lawn and adjacent shrub and flower beds are extensive. Lengths of hose lying about mar the appearance of lawns; no one is going to put away a hose that must be used the next day. Of course the best time to put in underground watering systems is before the major landscaping projects are under way, but actually they can be put in at any stage without too much fuss. There are reasonably priced kits available that a homeowner can install, sufficient for about a quarter acre of lawn and garden. Engineering and landscape contractors can also put in more complicated systems. Before making a decision, you or your contractor will want to be certain your water pressure is sufficient to operate efficiently the series of pop-up sprinklers which may be installed.

Work-saving plants

A number of plants can be as decorative and rewarding as many that require lots of attention. Most ground-cover plants are in this category, as are many of our most beautiful shrubs and trees. Among garden flowers, the daffodil and day-lily are examples of two plants that give much of themselves for little effort from us.

The plea has been made to save as many trees as possible that exist on your property before construction is started. This advice can apply to many other plants that may be present. Shrubs, wild flowers of many kinds (such as ferns, which are one of nature's own ground covers) may be in plentiful supply. If the time of year is fall or winter, or if you might not recognize the plants anyway, it still behooves you to restrain the bulldozer from completely clearing your land. Sooner or later, with the help of friends, neighbors, and books, you will find out what plants exist and which are worth saving. Wild-flower gardening in sun or shade requires little care — in fact the charm of a naturalistic area is in its casual, untampered-with appearance. (For more on wild-flower or woodland gardening, see page 130.)

Coping with pests

Pest control looms as the giant among maintenance problems, especially to new homeowners who imagine bugs and some form of pestilence lurk beneath every plant. Actually there are plants (the beautiful hybrid tea rose and delphinium are two examples) which harbor as well as attract more than their share of pests, but the majority of plants with which most homeowners are concerned are amazingly resistant — considering the number of garden pests one may find listed in books devoted to the subject. Many gardeners with small properties will find that they can get along for several seasons without worrying about the application of sprays or dusts, especially if they avoid certain "bug-catching" plants, such as the aforementioned hybrid tea rose and delphinium.

Of course there are years when troubles will appear. Typical might be a plague of cankerworms (often called inchworms), caterpillars attached to slender threads on which they seem to sail into one's property from all directions, ready to munch on all foliage within reach. The cankerworm and the alarming gypsy-moth caterpillar can be serious pests to shade trees in some years (and to conifers in the case of the gypsy moth), but conservation authorities are doubtful whether the cure, usually aerial spraying over extensive forested areas with a chemical such as Sevin, justifies the greater risk or possible damage to the total environment. In the meantime, scientists are attempting to find less drastic, more "natural" methods of coping with severe infestations of such pests.

During years when infestation is especially severe in entire communities, homeowners with wooded properties may elect to take individual action — the hiring of professionals with high-powered equipment to spray their trees, since amateurs with hand sprayers cannot possibly do a thorough job on tall trees. If you decide on this course, be sure the spray is applied at the proper time to control the pest and that the spraying is done by competent operators who use their equipment and poisonous materials with intelligence.

While most chemicals that kill insect pests are poisonous, some offer less danger to humans and warm-blooded animals and fewer hazards and disturbance to the environs than others. Among the least hazardous are rotenone, pyrethrum, and nicotine sulfate, old remedies eclipsed by the advent of the wonder chemicals but now once again being recommended to control most sucking insects as well as certain chewing pests. Among the newer chemicals considered less hazardous in the control of most garden pests are Sevin (carbaryl), Spectricide (diazinon), malathion, and methoxychlor.

Certain systemic insecticides (so-called because they are absorbed into the plant's system via roots or foliage, causing the plant to become toxic to pests that suck the plant juices), although generally very poisonous, are considered less hazardous than other insecticides. When used carefully according to directions, systemics are a lifesaver for a busy homeowner who wishes to control leaf-miners, which render the new foliage of birch trees so unsightly. Usually only two applications are required for perfect control of this disfiguring pest. Compare with the nuisance of measuring, preparing, and applying of a standard insecticide, which must be directed to every leaf to be effective and which must often be sprayed over the tree several times a season.

Most of the chemicals mentioned above are available from garden centers in aerosol cans, and for gardeners with small gardens, relying on aerosol bombs for occasional use makes good sense. They are easy to store, take up little shelf room, and are convenient and handy to use as no time need be spent in preparation. Of course they are more expensive than dusts or sprays bought in bulk form, but then to apply such materials you must first purchase a sprayer or duster.

You may decide, however, to dispense entirely with spraying or dusting with poisonous chemicals, a decision which lowers maintenance considerably, as fussing with balky spraying equipment (there is nothing more maddening to a gardener than to finally load his sprayer, then find that the spray head or nozzle is clogged!) can spoil half a day.

Organic gardening methods

Avoiding the use of poisonous chemicals in the garden is an ever-spreading practice, due in large part to the efforts of the late Rachel Carson and to increasing concern generally over our careless and exploitative use of the environment. However, it must be realized that "organic" gardeners may deserve first credit, as they have been preaching against the use of poisonous sprays and commercial (rather than natural) fertilizers for many years. It is of interest that many a canny organic gardener has known that growing marigold plants in his garden seems to control such soil pests as nematodes. Quite recently, this seeming bit of folklore was verified scientifically by experiments conducted at the Connecticut Agricultural Experiment Station. (Other plants which may act as bug repellents or killers include chives and geraniums for aphids, especially aphids on roses; onions for control of Mexican bean beetles, peach-tree borers, and aphids; and dill for cucumber beetles and stinkbugs.)

Another simple pest remedy recently announced is the use of beer to attract and trap slugs. Pour the beer into dishes that are accessible to the slugs and place them near vegetable and flowering plants.

Even beginners are aware of the worthy work accomplished by the ladybug or lady beetle, a small, orange flying beetle marked by dark spots. The beetles feed on soft-bodied insects such as aphids, various scales, weevils, mealybugs, and the Colorado potato beetle. Ladybugs can be purchased from western concerns and carefully liberated on various plants about the garden. Praying mantises — large, rather handsome green monsters — are also familiar to many gardeners and homeowners. They are also beneficial as they prey on aphids, caterpillars, flies, beetles, and other pests. If you wish to introduce the praying mantis to your property (or add to the existing population), it is possible to buy egg cases from Bio-Control Company, Route 2, Box 2397, Auburn, California 95602. The same company sells ladybugs.

One of the better known nonchemical methods for destroying grubs of the Japanese and Asiatic beetles is a bacterial control known as milky spore disease. The disease, which was first discovered on beetles in New Jersey in 1933, has become a standard treatment in beetle-infested turf, and is given much credit for the decline of this serious pest. (Home gardeners can purchase the disease spores, which are commercially known as "Doom," from Fairfax Biological Laboratories, Clinton Corners, New York 12514.)

A tried-and-true method of pest control is the removal of Japanese beetles, rose chafers (tan beetles found on roses and peonies in early summer), and various caterpillars from plants by hand and dropping them into jars of kerosene. Clusters of aphids and red spider mites (very tiny web-spinning spiders that suck plant juices, thereby giving the foliage a desiccated, brownish appearance) can be washed off plants with a strong jet of water from the hose.

Birds, of course, are of vital importance in the control of insects harmful to plants. Their presence in your garden can be encouraged by adequate shelter (trees and shrubs, especially evergreens in the winter), water for drinking and bathing (small, shallow pools or the usual bird baths), and certain fruiting plants, as well as feeding stations in winter when insects are scarce.

Moles and mice can be pesky in home gardens. Yet moles (which do not eat plant roots or bulbs, as do mice) are being observed more kindly nowadays, for they survive on Japanese-beetle grubs and other soil inhabitants; the French revere the mole for its ability to aerate heavy soil. However, few homeowners can regard the humped-up mole runs crisscrossing their lawns very benignly. And in gardens, moles can injure plants by creating air pockets between plant roots and soil. There are various recommended methods for ridding properties of moles, but you may find living with the mole easier! Among the usual controls are traps and gassing the runways. Certainly mole runs should be tramped down as soon as noticed. Ridding your soil of such mole food as grubs of Japanese beetles will send the moles elsewhere to forage for food. The aforementioned milky spore disease is an acceptable method for eliminating grubs, but it is a slow process, usually taking a few years. Less acceptable in this poison-conscious era but faster is the use of chemicals such as chlordane.

Perhaps the worst crime of the mole is that his runways can be taken over by field and pine mice. (The field mouse has a long tail; the pine mouse, a short tail.) Both are very destructive and are often the culprits when tulip and hyacinth bulbs disappear, when rose bushes, hollies, and other woody-stemmed plants fall over and upon examination show their entire root and stem area to have been chewed away. I know of no sure method for getting rid of these pests short of placing very toxic baits throughout the garden. Perhaps the least offensive means is still the cat! (Many bird lovers hesitate to keep cats, but they should be assured that the number of birds killed by cats is negligible compared to the numbers destroyed by man-caused catastrophes.) If you live in field-mouse country, you can reduce your anguish over the damage caused by these creatures by avoiding plants that comprise their favorite food: tulips, hyacinths, crocuses (but not daffodils), hybrid tea roses, hollies, lilies, dahlias, such vegetable crops as potato, carrot, shallot, and strawberry, and many perennials with swollen roots (bleeding-heart, babys-breath, for example). Another approach is to be lighthearted! Replace the plants as they are destroyed, knowing that rarely are all plants lost and that there are bound to be off years among these pests, just as there are for most insects and diseases. In other words, learn to live with the mice as well as with the moles!

Much of the same philosophy can apply to rabbits. If you discover that certain plants are consistently chewed off by rabbits all winter, protect them with a tent of fine mesh hardware cloth. Trunks of young fruit trees can be encircled with the same material to keep rabbits from gnawing at the bark. Where the rabbit population is heavy, it may be necessary to protect vegetable gardens with a fence. In small gardens and around favorite plants, a measure of control may result from using repellents in aerosol spray cans. They are found in garden centers and are listed by many mail-order nursery and seed concerns.

Color in a flower garden can begin early with such spring-blooming bulbs as tulips (which must be planted in the fall), and with perennials such as the ever-popular basket-of-gold (Alyssum saxatile), *which here tumbles over a low retaining wall.*

Flower garden in spring. Color at this season comes from a variety of plants including red tulips, the yellow euphorbia (a hardy relative of the more familiar poinsettia), and pansies. Other spring-flowering perennials are bleeding heart, candytuft, and such bulbs as hyacinths. Later-blooming plants—day-lily, phlox, peony—add to the effect with their clumps of fresh, new foliage. Plate 7

The same flower garden in summer. Early to mid-summer is the peak season for most flowering hardy plants. In the border of this garden the purple-blue flowers of gray-leaved catmint (Nepeta mussini) contribute mist-like color effects for a long period. The spikes of astilbe and yellow heads of yarrow are also effective. Phlox and day-lily plants carry display through the rest of the summer. Plate 8

Flowering crabapples are excellent trees for suburban properties—either as lawn subjects or as accents adjoining a terrace or patio area. They offer year-long interest, first, beautiful, fragrant flowers in midspring, then colorful fruits in late summer and fall, and finally, a picturesque branch silhouette during the winter. Plate 9

Favorite window box or planter combination is red geraniums and the trailing vinca, a tender relative of the hardy ground cover, myrtle. In this wooden planter a few plants of a ruffled white petunia have been included for contrast with the red geraniums, while touches of blue are given by the trailing annual, lobelia. Plate 10

Colorful, foolproof garden of annuals—marigolds and zinnias—avoids pitfalls for beginners. Such a planting can be decorative in a variety of situations so long as sunshine is plentiful for most of the day, and can provide ample material for indoor arrangements. Both plants are easy to grow from seed; or young plants can be purchased from garden centers. Plate 11

Outdoor-living areas can be as much garden as terrace when they are surrounded with colorful shrubs and other plants. This backyard terrace offers spring beauty from lilac and pink-flowered rhododendrons beneath a white-flowered dogwood. Later, both the dogwood and the lilac supply dappled shade from midday sunshine. Plate 12

Daffodils in drifts can be planted in home woodland properties of any size, to provide many weeks of spring color. The bulbs must be planted in the fall. Thereafter they survive for years with little care other than occasional fertilizing. Companions for daffodils include many kinds of wildflowers and such shrubs as rhododendrons. Plate 13

5 Ideas for Flower Gardens

The day of elaborate, huge flower gardens is over. Today, the labor shortage, the smaller size of properties, and the general mobility of most families have combined to make small gardens and limited plant groupings appealing and necessary. Small gardens offer ample scope for creativity for beauty and enjoyment, and can be even more challenging than the huge flower gardens that used to be the rule rather than the exception.

On small properties each plant must count in the over-all effect, whether it is a shrub which flowers only in the spring but has attractive foliage the rest of the summer, or a clump of bearded iris planted in an "island" in the terrace. The spring-flowering shrub can become the background for a dozen bright red petunias in summer; or if red and green is too obvious a color combination, choose white petunias, which are often especially fragrant. The clump of iris will be strikingly handsome in flower in early summer, but after the flowering period has passed, the sharply tapered blue-green leaves remain an interesting accent against the gray flagstone of the patio flooring. Further contrast can be achieved by a layer of white pebbles over the soil of the "island." Or a packet of sweet-alyssum seed could have been scattered around the iris in spring. Sweet-alyssum develops quickly from seed, and the plants begin to flower when only a few inches high. These are just two small garden ideas and, as you can see, involve only a few plants and a minimum of effort.

However, many homeowners, who find they appreciate and enjoy working with flowering plants, are not going to be satisfied with just a few sweet-alyssum plants or clumps of bearded iris. They want a more substantial, permanent flower garden, one in which several different kinds of annuals are used, or one that includes perennials, such as daylilies and summer phlox, along with the various annuals. This garden may resemble the herbaceous or perennial borders of yesterday in the ways that the plants are combined and contrasted with each other, but it will undoubtedly be much reduced in size and scope.

Requirements and locations for flower gardens

Most of the commonly grown flowering plants — annuals such as marigold, zinnia, and cosmos, and perennials such as chrysanthemum, phlox, and lupine — give their best performances in full sunshine, although many will tolerate a few hours or so of daily shade. Also important is soil that drains readily and does not remain waterlogged like a swamp.

Flower gardens and borders can run in front of shrub plantings, hedges, fences, walls, or along walks. Sometimes a corner of the property makes the best location.

Often the most logical place for a flower garden is along one or two sides of a rectangular patio or terrace adjacent to the house. Such a location guarantees maximum enjoyment of the flowers, as they can be appreciated by those within the house who gaze out and also by those who are using the terrace. The terrace flower garden can be of the most simple design, such as a border a few feet wide containing pink petunia and white sweet-alyssum plants, or yellow French marigolds edged with blue ageratum plants. If the garden receives a portion of daily shade — so desirable for most outdoor living areas — the plants can be selected from those which can endure several hours of shade yet still perform in a satisfactory manner. (Even petunia plants can endure a few hours of daily shade.) Shade-tolerant plants include impatiens, wax and tuberous-rooted begonias, the nontrailing vinca known as Madagascar periwinkle (*Vinca rosea*), fuchsia, and coleus, whose richly colored foliage more than compensates for the insignificant flower spikes.

The shapes of flower beds can vary according to their location and purpose in the landscape: a corner garden is usually roughly triangular; a border along one or two sides of a terrace will be rectangular or form an L and have straight rather than scalloped edges. Gardens along walks or in front of mixed shrubbery plantings may be ribbon-like with dips and curves which follow the lines of the walks or shrub background. Yet a flower garden with too many curves should be avoided:

Ideas for Flower Gardens

it can contribute an effect of fussy clutter to the small property and is always more difficult to maintain, as straight edges are easier to keep neat than those with frequent curves. Free-form shapes — kidney, teardrop, crescents — can also be considered for today's flower gardens and can be especially effective for low-growing plants which have been set out for mass-color displays.

One of the most successful summer flower gardens I have seen, and for all the world to enjoy, was located in the owner's front yard, extending the entire length — and on both sides — of a split-rail fence which separated the property from the road. A variety of annuals and perennials were on display, mostly in groupings of three to five plants, but with occasional larger and taller plants (such as the blue-flowered globe-thistle) set as accents against the fence. Among the plants were snapdragon, gladiolus (planted close together in groups of five or more, close to the fence rails), dahlia (the medium-height, profuse-flowering varieties rather than the very tall, mammoth-flowered kinds grown for exhibition in fall flower shows!), the bushy yellow Marguerite daisy, cosmos, both French and African varieties of marigold, zinnia, perennial or summer phlox, day-lily, and the tall, blue-flowered mealycup sage (*Salvia farinacea*). Bursts of flower color even draped the fence posts and extended along the rails, where large-flowered clematis in deep purple-blue shades had been planted at intervals.

The success of this old-fashioned border — old-fashioned because it was a mixture of many kinds of flowers, all selected for their profuse flowering habits — was in part due to its appropriateness to the split-rail fence. The fence, in turn, was the correct choice for the property and house, an attractive modern version of a Colonial farmhouse.

Permanent color from perennials

Perhaps the word "permanent" is too optimistic. Yet such well-known perennials as day-lily, summer phlox, iris, Oriental poppy, peony, chrysanthemum, and bleeding-heart have the advantage over annuals of lasting for several seasons, even if not forever. Once planted, most can remain in the same location for long periods before requiring renovation such as lifting and dividing. There are no special rules for the timing of this attention, but when a perennial begins to crowd its neighbors or itself, becomes more leafy than floriferous, or when the center of the

The old-fashioned doorway garden, especially appropriate for cottages, can be comforting and colorful — and easy if annual plants, such as marigold, ageratum, and zinnia, are used. Other suitable plants are sweet-alyssum, impatiens, wax begonia, geranium, petunia, flowering tobacco, and nasturtium.

clump dies, it is time to take spade or fork in hand and dig up the plant. Spring and fall are the best seasons. A plant such as the peony will not need dividing for years and years, but it is an exception; perennial aster and chrysanthemum benefit from dividing and resetting every spring, and the summer phlox about every third or fourth year.

It is up to you to decide which plant group — annuals or perennials — you choose to complete your flower garden, but most people find the ideal solution is to select from both groups, using them in combination with trees, shrubs, ground covers, and hardy bulbs.

Perhaps the most practical, modern way to use perennials is to give them more individual treatment, spreading one or a group as needed over many sections of the property. Day-lilies against a shrub planting; a dozen or so primroses and violas under a flowering dogwood tree; a hosta in a shaded nook of a terrace — these are only a few of the ways that perennial plants can be used in contemporary landscapes.

Long perennial borders, perhaps 100 feet in length and 8 to 12 feet wide, are rarely seen today except on estates and in public gardens, both because of the space they occupy and the high maintenance they require. There are virtually no everblooming perennials that can compare with the long flowering effect contributed by such annuals as the marigold or petunia, so keeping a fairly elaborate perennial garden in color over an entire summer is a challenge to even the most dedicated and experienced of gardeners.

Should you wish to plant a perennial garden, a compromise is possible by making a small, much reduced version of a grand border, and many gardeners do this with great success. Such a garden's dimensions can vary according to your space and ambition, but a minimum width of about 4 feet is necessary and 6 feet is better. A day-lily clump soon fills a 4-foot circle, so you can readily see why wider borders are necessary if you wish to achieve the step-down effect possible with tall or background plants, then those of middle range, and finally the lowest ones in the front. A pleasant 4-foot-wide border can be created by using an occasional large plant such as a day-lily, phlox, or bleeding-heart, but relying mostly on groups of such medium-sized and small perennials as viola, dianthus, and Shasta daisy, and annuals such as petunia and marigold.

Before you decide to plan and plant a garden of perennials, check the following observations and guidelines:

A perennial garden is not forever! Herbaceous plants rarely possess the permanence of woody plants such as trees and shrubs. A perennial garden should be regarded as an ever-changing, ever-changeable project. Plants will need shifting and dividing after a few years; others may not prosper at all, necessitating more changes. Your likes and dislikes for certain plants will change.

Flower gardens increase maintenance problems. Watering is necessary when rains fail. A few plants (such as the delphinium) require weekly spraying against persistent pests like the cyclamen mite. A few plants require staking or some support. Fading flowers should be removed, not only for the sake of the garden's appearance, but also to prevent seed formation. (Self-sown seedlings of such perennials as summer phlox can become a nuisance.) The old flowers of both the

112 Landscaping and the Small Garden

day-lily and the bearded iris detract from the beauty of the newly opened flowers on the same plants and should be removed daily. Many perennial plants spread rapidly and after a few years crowd less invasive neighboring plants, or fail to flower as abundantly, thus needing dividing and replanting. And finally there are weeds which must be ruthlessly checked throughout the season.

Decide in which part of the flowering season you wish peak bloom and plan accordingly. It is foolish to plan and plant a garden of perennials in which the major color effects are produced while the owners are away. The summer vacationer can plan a beautiful spring garden of such perennials as bleeding-heart, blue phlox, basket-of-gold, candytuft, doronicum, and trollius, augmented by bold groups of tulip, daffodil, and hyacinth. The city dweller who summers and gardens in the country can rely on later-flowering plants; pholx, bee-balm, yarrow, and many annuals.

Maintaining a succession of color. Without a corps of gardeners and extensive nursery beds, the average home gardener today cannot expect to keep vast sweeps of color from spring to fall in the entire flower garden — no matter what its size. Instead, there will be patches of color, sometimes quite concentrated if the gardener has selected mostly early summer perennials, along with fresh clumps of developing or mature greenery of varying tints and textures from plants that have not yet flowered or whose blooming season has already passed. Plants with gray foliage are always useful, as they provide a background for plants that are flowering, and are of interest themselves throughout the growing season. Few perennial plants possess a truly everblooming habit, although many have quite long blooming periods. (A healthy skepticism should be maintained toward nursery catalogues and advertisements which claim an "everblooming" habit for certain perennials.) There *are* perennials which flower for a part of every season. The trick is to find them, work out a few combinations here, an accent plant there, and thus enjoy some color in parts of the garden all through the growing season. Even in a small garden, the best effects in color and form from perennials are reached by planting each kind in groups of three or more. Certain perennials, such as the globe-thistle or peony, are large enough to stand alone, but the majority of perennials can be effective only in numbers. (For suggestions for specific combinations of flowering plants, see Small Garden Ideas and Plant Combinations, page 151. For blooming sequences of major flower-garden plants, consult the list that follows.)

Suggestions for flower garden color from spring to fall

EARLY TO MIDSPRING

Basket-of-gold (*Alyssum saxatile*), columbine (*Aquilegia* species and their varieties), English daisy, (*Bellis perennis*), bleeding-heart (*Dicentra spectabilis*), leopardbane (*Doronicum caucasicum*), yellow euphorbia (*Euphorbia epithymoides*), candytuft (*Iberis sempervirens*), dwarf bearded iris (*Iris pumila*), Virginia bluebells (*Mertensia virginica*), blue phlox (*Phlox divaricata*), primrose (*Primula* species and varieties), lungwort (*Pulmonaria saccharata*), globeflower (*Trollius asiaticus*), speedwell (*Veronica gentianoides*), pansy (*Viola*).

Also such bulbs as daffodil, tulip, and hyacinth, and many low-growing and mound-forming or spreading plants which are more often recommended for rock gardens but are quite satisfactory in the foreground of a border.

LATE SPRING

Grass pink (*Dianthus plumarius*), fringed bleeding-heart (*Dicentra eximia*), cranesbill (*Geranium grandiflorum*), sweet-rocket (*Hesperis matronalis*), bearded iris and Siberian iris varieties, catchfly (*Lychnis viscaria flore-pleno*), peony varieties. Also green and gray foliage of later maturing plants.

EARLY SUMMER

Yellow yarrow (*Achillea* 'Coronation Gold' and the like), wild-indigo (*Baptisia australis*), bellflower (*Campanula carpatica, C. persicifolia,* and others), painted daisy (*Chrysanthemum coccineum*), Shasta daisy *Chrysanthemum maximum*), delphinium (*Delphinium* hybrids), sweet William (*Dianthus barbatus*), gas-plant (*Dictamnus*), globe-thistle (*Echinops ritro*), cranesbill (*Geranium pratense*), early day-lily varieties (*Hemerocallis*), Japanese iris (*Iris kaempferi*), many kinds of lily (*Lilium*), lupine (*Lupinus* hybrids), bee-balm (*Monarda* hybrids), catmint (*Nepeta mussinii*), Oriental poppy (*Papaver orientale*), early varieties of summer phlox (*Phlox paniculata*), balloon-flower (*Platycodon grandiflorum*), mealycup sage (*Salvia farinacea*), blue sage (*Salvia* x *superba*), lamb's-ears (*Stachys olympica*), dusty meadow-rue (*Thalictrum glaucum*), Carolina-lupine (*Thermopsis caroliniana*), mullein (*Verbascum chaixii*), speedwell (*Veronica incana* and *Ver-*

onica spicata). Also as background and nearby accents: floribunda and hybrid tea rose varieties, shrub rose varieties, mock-orange (*Philadelphus*), clematis (on trellis), and such annuals as French marigold, petunia, and dwarf zinnia varieties for the foreground of the garden.

MIDSUMMER TO FALL

Monkshood (*Aconitum*), butterfly-weed (*Asclepias tuberosa*), aster or Michaelmas daisy (*Aster* species and varieties), boltonia (*Boltonia* species), chrysanthemum (*Chrysanthemum* varieties), sea-holly (*Eryngium*), babys-breath (*Gypsophila paniculata*), Helen's-flower (*Helenium autumnale*), midseason-to-late day-lily varieties (*Hemerocallis*), gayfeather (*Liatris* species), sea-lavender (*Limonium latifolium*), loosestrife (*Lythrum* 'Morden's Pink' and the like), mid-season-to-late varieties of summer phlox (*Phlox paniculata*), false-dragonhead (*Physostegia virginiana*), stonecrop (*Sedum spectabile*), redhot poker (*Tritoma* hybrids), speedwell (*Veronica longifolia*), Spanish-bayonet (*Yucca filimentosa*). Also such annuals as the taller African marigold, cosmos, nicotiana, zinnia.

Note: Foliage accents throughout the season include rue (*Ruta graveolens*), various wormwood species (*Artemisia*), lamb's-ears (*Stachys olympica*), various stonecrops (*Sedum*), cotton-lavender (*Santolina*), iris, day-lily, and yarrow (*Achillea*).

Temporary color with annuals and summer bulbs

Annual plants give the biggest and quickest splashes of color for summer gardens. They are the answer for those who like to experiment with color and who like to change their schemes each year. Annuals are also fine plants for the vacation home, as they can be planted late in spring or early summer and will still give bloom before frost cuts them down. In mild climates, many annuals act more like perennial plants, giving months and months of color. For the new homeowner, they are a boon for the period before final landscaping plans have been started or completed. They can be used to cover bare ground before shrubs have been planted or before they have reached an effective size.

When annuals are grown from seed, they are more economical than when they are purchased as plants from florists or garden centers. Annuals almost always cost less than the longer lasting perennials.

Other temporary color effects can be had with tender, bulb-like plants such as the dahlia, gladiolus, tuberous begonia, Peruvian-daffodil, and tuberose. In mild-climate gardens, these plants can usually remain in place for several years. In northern areas, their roots or tubers are started into growth in spring or early summer. They must be lifted in the fall and stored over winter in frost-free but cool shelter. Many northern gardeners consider them expendable in the fall and buy new plants the following spring.

Together, annuals and tender summer-blooming bulbs offer homeowners tremendous flexibility in adding color to their properties. Drab color combinations are no more to be tolerated in the garden today than in homes. The same possibilities for lively color effects exist outdoors. Colors in new varieties of such popular plants as petunia, impatiens, zinnia, coleus, and marigold are brighter than they used to be, and their range has been extended. Impatiens and petunia varieties of neon color intensity are available to brighten gardens from spring to fall. For the spur-of-the-moment person who wants an immediate effect, potted plants of petunia, marigold, geranium, ageratum, and zinnia can be picked out at the nearest garden center, and within hours can be popped into the ground. If the soil has been previously readied — that is, spaded over and raked after a commercial fertilizer has been sprinkled over the surface (follow directions on the fertilizer container, as brands and formulas can differ in the rates of application) — the project can be accomplished in jiffy time. As a matter of fact, there are plant pots, made of pressed peat and called "jiffy" pots, which speed up the planting project, as both pot and plant are inserted in the soil. The roots of the plant soon grow through the peat pot as it disintegrates in the soil. One final step you should never shirk: thoroughly water the newly set plants and surrounding soil.

Ten major annuals for reliable, long-season color

AGERATUM (*Ageratum*) — Unexcelled for edging. Fluffy flower heads are in various shades of violet-blue or white, soon forming rolling carpets of color. Plants develop slowly from seed; sow seeds early indoors according to directions on seed packets, or buy plants at a garden center. Heights: 3 to 6 inches. Sun or light shade. *Not* drought-resistant — may need daily watering during dry weather.

116   *Landscaping and the Small Garden*

COSMOS (*Cosmos*) — Tall plants for cutting and display, best grown in combination with other annuals such as marigold and zinnia. White, rose, dark red, or pink flowers and filmy foliage. Also orange and yellow flowers from Klondike cosmos varieties. Heights: 4 to 5 feet; about 2½ feet for Klondike cosmos. For sun.

FLOWERING TOBACCO OR NICOTIANA (*Nicotiana affinis*) — Delightfully fragrant white, rose, or dark red flowers in racemes. Heights: 2½ to 3 feet. Sun or light shade.

IMPATIENS (*Impatiens* hybrids) — Hybridizers have done wonders with this old-fashioned favorite. Colors include a full range except for blue, purple, and yellow. A splendid plant for massing for even color. Start seed early indoors, or buy plants at a garden center. Heights: 6 to 15 inches. Sun or partial shade.

MARIGOLD (*Tagetes*) — Many forms, tall, medium, and low, with giant to button-sized flowers in yellow, orange, and rust range. An all-marigold garden can be an eye stopper! Heights: 8 to 40 inches. For sun.

NASTURTIUM (*Tropaeolum*) — Quick to bloom (one month from seed) and tolerant of hot sun and lean soil. Soak seeds in a tumbler of water overnight before sowing. Try a few leaves in a mixed salad! Rich colors. Trailing types fine in raised planters and window boxes. Heights: 12 inches. For sun.

PETUNIA (*Petunia*) — Perhaps the most versatile and beautiful of modern annual plants. Suitable for planters, window boxes, hanging boxes, or baskets as well as borders and among a mixture of plants. Fine color range in single and double flowers, often deliciously scented. Be sure to plant some white petunias near or on the patio for evening enjoyment. The petunia is slow to develop from seed; start plants indoors according to instructions on the packet, or buy plants. Petunia plants and seed packets are often more expensive than other annuals. Heights: 6 to 15 inches. Sun or light shade.

SNAPDRAGON (*Antirrhinum majus*) — Really a tender perennial, and in cold climates plants generally do not survive winter. Handsome and substantial spikes in yellow, coral, red, rust, pink, and rose. Plants develop slowly from seed; start seeds indoors in late winter or buy plants from garden centers. Heights: 8 to 36 inches. Sun.

Ideas for Flower Gardens 117

SWEET-ALYSSUM (*Lobularia maritima*) — One of the easiest plants to grow from seed — just scatter the seeds over the soil where you want them to bloom — with a long flowering period. If plants show the strain of their tremendous flower production at midsummer, just take your scissors and shear the tops of the plants. This will result in a new flurry of bloom which should last well into the autumn. Flowers are white and usually fragrant; also rose and violet varieties. Heights: 3 to 6 inches. Sun.

ZINNIA (*Zinnia*) — Nearly as versatile as the marigold and petunia for modern gardens. Wide color range and flower form. The ball-flowered Thumbelina and Peter Pan zinnia varieties, at 6 to 8 inches in height, are excellent for low borders. All zinnia varieties develop quickly from seed planted in the garden in midspring. Heights: 6 to 30 inches. For sun.

Hardy spring-flowering bulbs for generous color with little effort

High on the list of low-maintenance plants are the spring-flowering bulbs, which can be counted on to provide masses of cheering color when northern gardens have almost despaired of spring's arrival. Daffodils, especially, and many of the "little" bulbs, such as glory-of-the-snow (*Chionodoxa*) and scilla, give many weeks of color in the spring, the only effort required by the gardener being to plant the bulbs in the fall. They can remain in place for several seasons before needing such attention as dividing or fertilizing. The little bulbs will often self-sow.

Tulips and hyacinths are also splendid bulbs for spring color. In the south and in mild climates, their bulbs must be refrigerated for several weeks before planting, unless pretreated bulbs are offered by the dealer. They give the best performance the first spring after planting; thereafter the bulbs begin to split and flowers become smaller.

For inspiration on where and how to use the spring-flowering bulbs, American gardeners have only to look to the Dutch. The gardeners of the Netherlands not only know how to grow bulbs (most of the bulbs sold in this country are imported from the Netherlands), but also are experienced in creating beautiful spring gardens with them. A showplace for the Dutch skill in plant growing and landscaping is Keukenhof Gardens, a sixty-acre park in Lisse which is open to the public during

118   *Landscaping and the Small Garden*

the spring season. There are formal and informal gardens that feature spring bulbs in every setting imaginable — woodlands, terraces, pool- and waterside plantings, rock gardens, walls, walks, borders. The bulbs are displayed along with appropriate companion plants, such as evergreens, flowering shrubs, trees, and spring-blooming perennials. Every American who has visited Keukenhof Gardens has returned full of inspiration and fortified with concrete ideas on how to use bulbs around his own property, whether he owns several acres or less than a half.

During the next fall planting season, look around your own garden. You will see many ways to use bulbs. Among daffodils, freely scatter the bulbs of low-growing crocus, glory-of-the-snow, scilla, and grape-hyacinth. In a corner or in front of shrubs, one or two bleeding-heart plants, a dozen or so pink tulips, and several pansy plants in the foreground make a charming small garden. Later, annuals such as impatiens, petunia, and flowering tobacco (*Nicotiana*) can continue the color sequence.

If you have a flower border which is composed of spring-blooming perennials — blue phlox (*Phlox divaricata*), leopardbane (*Doronicum*), basket-of-gold (*Alyssum saxatile*), primrose (*Primula*) — adding at least three different varieties of tulips (in bold groups of ten or so) will enrich and ennoble the color effects of the entire garden.

Ten hardy bulbs for spring and summer

(*Note*: The following bulbs are planted in the fall)

CROCUS (*Crocus*) — 2 to 4 inches. Jaunty, cheering, and beautiful in both the bud and flower stage. Crocuses are probably the most beloved of the little spring bulbs. They are reasonable enough in price so the new homeowner, who may be "feeling the pinch" when faced with the prospect of buying shrubs or trees, can splurge. Crocus corms (similar to a bulb) can be purchased as mixed varieties to give a rich color range (white, yellow, lavender, purple, brown, and bicolor effects), or can be selected by color or by named species and varieties. Use them everywhere — under trees, shrubs, just off a terrace where they can be enjoyed from indoors, along a frequently traveled walk, by entrances, steps, against rocks, or in the lawn. (If you plant bulbs in grass, remember that early mowing must be postponed, as the foliage of all bulbs must ripen first, thus feeding the bulb in preparation for next year's flowers.)

Crocus flowers are amazingly hardy and impervious to late winter

Ideas for Flower Gardens 119

snowstorms. During inclement weather, the flowers simply close, unfolding again as conditions improve. In northern regions, it is possible to have some kind of crocus in bloom from late February or early March (depending on location) through the entire spring season.

DAFFODIL (JONQUIL OR NARCISSUS) (*Narcissus*) — 4 to 5 inches and up to 24 inches or so, depending on variety. One of the most popular spring-flowering bulbs offering tremendous variety in flower size and shape. Daffodil colors run to yellow, gold, and white with touches of orange, rusty red, or pink. The so-called pink daffodils have pink-tinted cups or centers with surrounding white petals (technically called a perianth). There are many kinds — all suitable for spring gardens among other plants, or for naturalizing in lawn areas or in woodlands among wild flowers. The smaller species, which may be 6 inches or less high, as in the case of the dainty "yellow hoop petticoat" (*N. bulbocodium*), are fine in rock gardens. You can choose early, midseason, or late varieties; 'February Gold,' 'March Sunshine,' and 'Peeping Tom' are examples of

Spring-flowering bulbs provide inexpensive, foolproof garden color for the small or large property alike. The bulbs, especially daffodils, can be naturalized in large drifts, or, as with this batch of ten or so tulip bulbs, planted in small pockets in a terrace.

exceptionally early varieties, usually in full bloom the first part of April on Long Island. Late varieties (mid-May or later, depending on season and region) include 'Frigid' and the magnificent 'Kilworth,' a large-flowered variety with an orange-red center surrounded by a bold perianth. Daffodils can become a hobby unto themselves. Once planted, the bulbs can remain in place for several seasons before they become so crowded as to impede flower production, then needing lifting and dividing. Mice will pass them by and the bulbs are generally free from pests and diseases.

FLOWERING ONION OR ALLIUM (*Allium*) — 1½ to 4 feet tall, depending on kind. There many species, offering tremendous contrast and diversity, although some are decidedly more showy in flower than others. Most gardeners are familiar with at least one flowering onion: the chive plants of herb gardens, which while in full bloom in early summer, are a most attractive sight. One of the spectacular flowering onions is *A. giganteum*, with 6-inch purple flower heads that float like balloons above 4-foot stems. The flowers are long lasting and provide considerable color in a most dramatic fashion in early summer flower gardens. Even larger flower heads are produced by *A. albopilosum*. Single star-shaped flowers combine to make a 10-inch head, carried on 2-foot stems, the effect being not unlike the burst from night fireworks displays. Some of the other flowering onions are less conspicuous, and are small enough to be planted in the soil pockets of rock gardens. The more flamboyant species, especially those mentioned above, are too big for most rock gardens but several plants can be grouped in shrubbery bays or among other perennials.

GLORY-OF-THE-SNOW OR CHIONODOXA (*Chionodoxa luciliae*) — 5 inches. One of the "little" bulbs of spring. Its lovely blue, pink, or white flowers are star-shaped and appear in midspring. The bulbs are standard favorites for scattering wherever early spring color can be enjoyed: in the lawn, under trees or in front of shrubs, among daffodils and early tulips, in rock gardens, or clustered around rocks or near steps.

HYACINTH (*Hyacinthus*) — 1 to 1½ feet. Heavy spikes of pendulous, bell-shaped flowers, waxy in texture, and in white, rose, pink, cerise, blue-lavender, lilac, and yellow. Hyacinths are lush beauties, which can appear symmetrical and formal; or, sadly, rather blowzy and untidy when the heavy flower heads are too much for the stems and they topple

Crocuses, among the earliest to appear of all spring bulbs, are small enough to be tucked in soil pockets among these stone steps. The blossoms, which simply close up when the weather is inclement, last for weeks.

over, subjecting the lovely flowers to mud staining from spring rains. Yet they are worth growing, if only for their exquisite fragrance. You can grow hyacinths in formal beds of triangular, rectangular, or oval shapes, a rather old-fashioned method but decidedly worth reviving today. There is no better way to dramatize the fresh greenness of a well-cared-for lawn, and, of course, the surrounding lawn is a perfect backdrop for the bright-colored hyacinths.

After flowering, the hyacinths can be discarded and annuals put in their place. Hyacinths can be grown in combination with tulips. Pansies, primroses, and English daisies are also fine companions, as are many other spring-flowering perennials. Some lovely colors have been introduced in hyacinths. The variety 'Orange Boven' has salmon-colored flowers; 'Princess Irene' has silvery pink flowers; 'Yellow Hammer' is more creamy in its color effect than yellow.

LILY (*Lilium*) — 2 to 5 feet, depending on species and variety. Although lily bulbs are planted in the fall, the flowers of most kinds appear in

122 Landscaping and the Small Garden

summer. The trumpet- or funnel-shaped flowers, usually large and on tall stems, can be impressive among other summer-flowering plants, such as phlox, liatris, babys-breath, Shasta daisies, and day-lilies. Or they can be scattered in groups in the foreground of shrubs. There are a few lilies that are suitable for the partial shade of woodland gardens. Many lilies are temperamental and their bulbs often disappear for no apparent reason. (One cause may be mice, which are very fond of the bulbs.) Many of the new lily hybrids from Oregon are disease-resistant and prove to be long lasting in the garden. 'Enchantment' is one such introduction. Its cup-shaped flowers are intensely red and are borne abundantly on 3-foot stems in early summer. (Many of the other Oregon hybrid lilies are very tall, making them difficult subjects for most small gardens.) If you are planning a long, mixed-flower border, you will certainly want to include some of these Oregon lilies for summer bloom. Many lilies are also fragrant.

PUSCHKINIA (*Puschkinia scilloides*) — 5 inches. Delicate, pale-blue bell-shaped flowers on slender stems. Another "little" spring bulb. Plant it with a free hand; among crocuses and daffodils, under and around forsythia, or with daffodils for a sky-blue-and-yellow color combination. These little bulbs will self-sow and spread freely. Once introduced into the garden, they will never leave.

SCILLA (OR SQUILL OR BLUEBELLS) (*Scilla*) — 8 to 24 inches. Several bell- or star-shaped flowers to a stem. The early-flowering scillas are similar to glory-of-the-snow in effect; the May-flowering bluebells (*S. endymion*) are taller and look more like miniature hyacinths. Within both groups, there are white, pink, and blue varieties. Plant them among the other small bulbs or naturalize in woodlands or in the lawn.

SNOWDROP (*Galanthus nivalis*) — 6 inches. Pendulous, snow-white flowers with distinct green tips on each petal. Just about the earliest of the little spring bulbs, with blooms sometimes appearing in January or February in mild winters or when the bulbs are planted in very protected situations. Plant snowdrops close together — the usual recommendation is so close that the bulbs touch each other. Snowdrops are perhaps more of a novelty than a necessity to most homeowners, but if you enjoy your garden in winter, you will certainly want to include several plantings about your property. Similar is the snowflake (*Leucojum vernum*), but its flowers are larger and appear later, usually with late crocus varieties.

Spring bulbs, such as tulips, make excellent front-yard plantings, especially among young shrubs along house foundations which have not yet filled out. The bulbs can be discarded after flowering, and their space filled by annuals such as petunia or marigold. The edging plant in front of these tulips is creeping thyme, a perennial.

TULIP (*Tulipa*) — 8 to 30 inches, depending on species and variety. Sculptured beauty in a magnificent array of colors describes the modern tulip. While the true tulip species generally remain diminutive and distinctive with many kinds remaining most suitable to rock gardens, the various hybrids of these species as well as the popular Darwin, cottage, and lily-flowered varieties are most representative of the modern tulip. Its garden value is tremendous, and prices remain within budget limits of most homeowners and gardeners. If you have not space enough for an all-tulip garden (see suggestions above under hyacinths), plant the bulbs in groups of a half dozen or a dozen among other perennials that flower in spring, such as the blue phlox (*Phlox divaricata*); or plant a double row around one or two sides of a terrace; or contrast tulips against shrubs or hedges or walls or fences. There are so many ways to use tulips in even the smallest garden that there is no reason for not enjoying their beauty at close hand. (Mice will, unfortunately, eat the bulbs; then the solution is to plant more bulbs, as the mice rarely devour all of them!) One thing about tulips: the bulbs are effective for only a few seasons before they split and then produce few and inferior flowers. Many homeowners have decided to treat tulips like annuals — plant them every year for best results.

Flower color in the shade

While great sweeps or masses of color are less common in shade (rare in deep shade — more likely in partial or high shade where there is good light and sometimes filtered sunshine for a part of the day), many color effects are possible, as has already been suggested. The all-green garden, in which tree and shrub forms and textures combine to make an acceptable substitute for flower color, except for seasonal color accents mostly in the spring, is one solution. The shrubs can include leucothoë, andromeda (*Pieris*), holly, and boxwood, as well as such low-growing plants as ferns, English ivy, wintercreeper, pachysandra, and myrtle. For strong color effects in spring, add rhododendron, azalea, and camellia, ajuga, lily-of-the-valley, and Christmas-rose. In partial shade, use tuberous and wax begonia, impatiens, fuchsia, achimenes (the last two are fine in hanging baskets on shaded terraces), day-lily, annual periwinkle (*Vinca rosea*), and sweet rocket.

Many spring-flowering native plants common to woodlands have colorful flowers. They include trillium, bloodroot, violet, blue phlox, columbine, and many others. Certain other plants suitable for shady gardens contribute unusual or colorful foliage, and include the tender bulb-like plants caladium and elephant's-ears; the tender coleus, which is grown as an annual; the perennials, hosta, many ferns and bergenia.

6 Gardens of Special Plants and for Special Interests

Herb gardening

The increase in growing herbs at home has kept pace with the rising interest in good food and its preparation. For casual kitchen use, a few herb plants can be tucked here and there about the garden — in the foreground of shrub groupings or in a convenient area near the kitchen door — but this is not taking advantage of the tremendous decorative qualities inherent in most herb plants.

Basil, in either its bright green or purple-leaved variety 'Dark Opal', is an example of an easy-to-grow annual herb as ornamental as it is useful. Another attractive herb is rosemary, a tender shrubby plant, which is appropriate on the patio in a large pot. Patio gardens along the Mediterranean would not be without it or without lavender, an aromatic herb valued in sachets.

Where space permits and you, the gardener, have the interest, there is no more pleasant and challenging way to grow herbs than in an all-herb garden of geometric shapes, patterns, and circles, often with intricate arrangements of plants once so common in the Elizabethan and Stuart knot gardens. Such gardens hardly have a low-maintenance rating, as the plants must be clipped and grown to perfection to maintain the pattern. More modest versions of such gardens are quite possible, and are far more practical for most of us today. They can be part of or adjacent to an outdoor living area, just about the only requirement being a fully sunny exposure, which is needed by the majority of herbs.

A fairly simple circular herb garden is possible with only a few kinds of herbs. It can be planted in a large soil pocket left in a terrace. Follow a "wheel" pattern, using the gray-foliaged santolina as the "spokes," with the spaces between filled by parsley, oregano, basil, sweet marjoram, savory, and chervil, the number of different herbs depending on the number of spaces between the "spokes." All but the santolina can easily be grown from seed; you will want to buy the santolina plants from a nursery or garden center. Or you might prefer to substitute chives for the santolina, as chives are inexpensive and easily divided. The wheel "rim" can be a border of thyme or teucrium, parsley, or more chives.

Other decorative ways to grow herbs is simply to leave the plants in pots — large earthenware or clay pots are especially suitable on brick-surfaced patios — and arrange them in attractive groupings along steps or on terraces or patios. The herbs most suited for this treatment are rosemary (large plants can be pruned to keep them shapely), lemon-verbena, tarragon, and true myrtle (*Myrtus communis*), but actually any herbs in pots can make an attractive picture. Obviously, unhealthy, neglected plants will mar the arrangement, no matter how intriguing their pots or how appropriate they are to their surroundings. If you are unable to give the plants the proper maintenance time — watering *before* the plants wilt and occasional booster applications of liquid fertilizer — pass this idea by and take on something you can more adequately handle. Larger pots do not dry out as fast as small ones; planters, tubs, and window-box-like containers retain moisture longer than most clay pots. Attractive as well as serviceable herb plant collections can be arranged in wooden planters built to fit the side dimensions of your deck or terrace area.

Among the most useful herbs that possess decorative properties too are lavender, parsley, chives, basil, mint, and sage. Lavender is a shrub-like perennial, which can grow quite large in mild climates, but in most northern areas remains around 24 inches or so in height. French lavender has green foliage and is only suitable for mild climates; English lavender has gray foliage and slender spikes of bluish, deep violet flowers. Even the dullest nose will respond to the clean, aromatic fragrance found in both foliage and flowers. Lavender is equally suitable for planting in all-herb gardens or among other flowers, but it can be straggly unless carefully cut back almost to old wood in the spring. Modern gardeners may find they receive the most value from lavender by tucking a plant here and there near steps, along walkways, or near

This semi-formal herb garden is enclosed by a clipped hedge. Informal borders of various herbs surround a rectangular central bed where the herbs are arranged in a more precise pattern. Herb gardens are essentially gardens of foliage, their color and effect coming from the grays and greens of the leaves and their varying textures.

entrances — anywhere so its refreshing scent can be enjoyed by passers-by.

One of the most delicate-flavored members of the onion tribe is chives, a plant worth having for its abundant lilac flowers in early summer. If you do not plan a major herb-garden effort, simply plant several clumps of chives among other flowers or in the foreground of a shrub planting. You will be pleased with their decorative effect, but you can also snip the leaves all summer to add to sour cream, cottage or cream cheese, or to any dish that will be improved by a mild onion flavor.

Clumps of chives are decorative in or out of bloom and make an attractive border for paths in vegetable gardens. After flowering, the faded heads can be cut off. The leaves can be snipped from spring to late fall for culinary use in a variety of recipes. A popular use is in sour cream.

One of the most foolproof herbs to grow from seeds is basil. Several varieties are available, differing slightly in size and leaf color and texture. Quite different in leaf color is 'Dark Opal,' a purple-leaved variety which contrasts handsomely with the fresh green foliage of the other basils. All basils are decorative enough to be grown in tubs or pots, among other herbs in planters, or among annual flowering plants such as marigold and sweet-alyssum. Basil is an essential ingredient to any cook who makes Italian dishes, and it is the best possible companion for tomatoes, whether sliced and served on a platter, or broiled or stewed. Fresh basil's licorice-like aroma and flavor are far more satisfying than the dried product bought in grocery stores. And home-dried basil is superior to most store offerings!

Parsley is such a taken-for-granted kitchen herb that its ornamental possibilities are often overlooked. Well-grown clumps of both the

Gardens of Special Plants and for Special Interests 129

curly and plain-leaved varieties make crisp, neat borders for any kind of garden. Parsley is easily grown from seed and can be sown in slight furrows where the plants are to remain. Or young plants can be carefully transplanted after a few leaves have appeared. Larger plants do not transplant as successfully as do most herb seedlings, as each plant has a taproot that resents being disturbed. The seed should be started in early spring. Vegetable gardeners often sow parsley and radish seed in the same row; the faster germinating radish will mark the row of parsley seed, which may take a few more weeks before germinating. Soaking the seed overnight before sowing is supposed to hasten germination.

The aim of the owners was to retain as much of the original woodland and its inherent naturalness as possible. The terrace in front of the owner-built retaining wall has been paved in random fashion with broken concrete sections and flat stones. Creeping thyme grows among the stones. Early spring color in the woods comes from daffodils and the small native white-flowered tree called shadblow (Amelanchier).

The hardy sage, with its characteristic pungent and silvery leaves, is a perennial, and, once planted (you can plant seeds or buy plants), should be around for several seasons. It is a tall plant, usually too coarse for small, precise herb plantings, but is fine in the background, especially among flowering plants. There are sages with green and yellow or purplish foliage which have decorative possibilities. Pineapple sage is a tender relative which will not survive winters outdoors in northern regions. Its leaves have a delicious fruit-like fragrance, and for this a plant or two is worth growing in a large pot on a terrace. In the fall, cut back straggly top growth — pineapple sage can grow 2 to 3 feet high — and place the potted plant in a cool, bright window. This is the only way to carry over the plants in cold climates — and you will enjoy the fragrant foliage all winter.

The various kinds of mints may seem too mundane to include, but they certainly have their culinary place, if only to garnish summer drinks. Mint likes slightly damp, rich soil and light shade. There are several kinds besides spearmint — apple-mint and curly-mint are two — which are freshly aromatic and pleasing to the eye because of their leaf textures. In the small garden, it is quite true that spearmint and the other kinds of mints must be planted where they will not become a nuisance. If you have a shaded terrace, try growing the various kinds of mints in large pots.

As your interest in herb gardening develops, you may wish to look up some of the old and not-so-old books on the subject. Many of the older books contain plans and patterns for knot gardens which can be adapted for today's gardens.

The wild-flower garden

You may be one of the fortunate new homeowners whose surrounding property contains trees which were present prior to building operations. No matter whether you have only a few trees or are blessed with a small-scale forest, such wooded areas provide welcome shade for your new home and terrace as well as near-natural opportunity for the creation of a wild-flower garden, one of the most satisfying experiences in the world of gardening. It has the added advantage of involving as much — or as little — effort as you, the new homeowner, wish to expend. It can be completed in one or two seasons, or it can become a pleasant pastime for all seasons. A woodland garden can be a modest project

Gardens of Special Plants and for Special Interests 131

limited to the most accommodating of native plants clustered under a few trees or large shrubs, or it can involve an entire property with as many kinds of native plants as you wish.

Preserving the trees and accompanying growth of a property has special meaning today because of emphasis on the original environment and the conservation of natural beauty. Establishing a wild-flower garden around your own home is a modest way of becoming personally involved with the problems of conservation.

On many properties, a wild-flower garden project may be well on the way because of the prior existence of many desirable plants native to the region. Much depends on the way the builder handled the land as he was constructing the house. Desirable native plants may be found along the property's boundaries or especially close to trees.

A problem for beginners may be recognition of native plants encountered on their own property or in nearby areas. A solution is to purchase an illustrated wild-flower handbook. Good ones include *A Field Guide to Wildflowers of Northeastern and North-central North America* by Roger Tory Peterson and Margaret McKenny and a companion volume, *A Field Guide to Rocky Mountain Wildflowers* by John J. Craighead, Frank C. Craighead, Jr. and Ray J. Davis (Houghton Mifflin Company, $4.95), as well as many others, most of which are devoted to the native plants of a state or region. These handbooks are not only essential for identification, but will give tips on culture by describing the plants' preferences in habitat.

You will find that the best source for most of the plants in your woodland garden will be the nurseries which specialize in native plants. Even general mail-order nurseries often offer a selection of native material, especially among ferns. Of course indiscriminate digging of plants from private properties, whose owners are concerned over conservation, or from sanctuaries is completely contrary to the conservation code, but collecting plants from roadsides or other areas that are subject to mowing or construction is permissible and well within the true spirit of conservation. Spring or fall are ideal plant-collecting seasons, especially after an earth-soaking rain. Pop the plants into plastic bags to prevent their roots from drying, and replant as quickly as possible.

The wild-flower garden may be a small one, perhaps an irregularly shaped "island" shaded by two or three trees. In more extensively wooded areas, a path or series of paths can be marked out. They should meander a bit in much the same fashion as do woodland trails you may have wandered along in Maine or Michigan. Surfacing the paths with pine bark, pine needles, sawdust, or wood chips makes them more attractive to look at as well as inviting to walk upon. As these materials break down from wear and the process of decay, they can be replaced. The resulting humus can always be transferred into planting areas for use as a mulch and soil conditioner. The trees themselves will play a part in the layout of paths. If your property is heavily wooded, an occasional tree may have to be removed, as will lower branches of some trees to improve the vista and to create "high" shade, so that light and even filtered sun or patches of sunshine can penetrate the home forest.

Underbrush and seedling trees must be thinned and removed. Certain native vines — Virginia creeper, catbrier, for instance — are effective plants for some locations, but they can get quickly out of control and smother choice wild flowers. (You must grub out their roots, because after being cut back, most woody weeds spring back the stronger!) If native shrubs are not in the area, you may want to add a few. The oak-leaf hydrangea (*Hydrangea quercifolia*), native viburnums, summersweet (*Clethra alnifolia*), and several kinds of native deciduous azaleas are all suitable. (Other shrubs can be found among the broad-leaved evergreens described on page 46.)

In most home woodland gardens, large-scale soil preparation, such as is associated with the establishment of a lawn or perennial garden, is neither desirable nor necessary. (An exception might be when the builder has dumped subsoil, usually inhospitable to the growth of woodland plants, in the area and has even raised the ground level around tree trunks.) Usually the soil can be prepared section by section as your planting plans progress. Special soil conditions occasionally must be provided for some plants, but the majority of woodland plants prefer an acid, humus-rich soil which does not remain soggy, yet retains a reasonable degree of moisture. Ideally some clay should be present; very sandy soils, even when they have been improved with the addition of peat moss, will require extra watering.

In areas where falling leaves have been accumulating for years to form layers of leafmold, the only effort required by the gardener is to lightly fork over the planting section, dig holes, and set out the plants. When the soil is sandy or the other extreme — too heavy — more effort is necessary to prepare the humus-rich soil so vital to most native plants. Mix in peat moss in sufficient quantity so that you can "feel" with your heads the improved texture of the original soil. (Other sources of humus are rotted sawdust or decayed wood chips, leafmold collected from a nearby area, or any decomposed material you may have access to.)

Gardens of Special Plants and for Special Interests 133

Most woodland plants are more effective in colonies — usually the the way they grow in nature. A small garden, such as the "island" mentioned earlier, might include a few taller accents, such as the interrupted fern. (*Osmunda claytoniana*), several kinds of trillium (the white *Trillium grandiflorum* is especially handsome), American columbine (*Aquilegia canadensis*) and Virginia bluebells (*Mertensia virginica*), for a red, white, and blue midspring color scheme. Additional plants might include Jack-in-the-pulpit (*Arisaema triphyllum*) and such ferns as the Christmas fern (*Polystichum acrostichoides*) or the lovely maidenhair (*Adiantum pedatum*).

In the larger woodland garden, the choice widens to the ever-fascinating May-apple (*Podophyllum peltatum*), foamflower (*Tiarella cordifolia*), and even the skunk-cabbage (*Symplocarpus foetidus*). The last is associated with wetlands, but it adapts to drier soil rich in humus. It is a fascinating plant to watch as its development keeps pace with that of spring — first, the strange flowers as snows recede, then the unfolding and growth of the foliage.

The strikingly beautiful red cardinal-flower (*Lobelia cardinalis*) and its relative, the great blue lobelia (*L. syphilitica*), flower over a long period in summer, and are handsome subjects along brooks (if you are blessed with such!) or beside any man-made pools. The closed or bottle gentian (*Gentiana andrewsii*) may lack the fragile beauty of the fringed gentian (*G. crinita*), a biennial which must be painstakingly grown from seed, yet it is a lovely perennial for autumn color. Some of the native plants which bloom in spring offer interest in the fall with their berries. Such a plant is Jack-in-the-pulpit, which has eye-catching clusters of bright scarlet fruits. False Solomon's-seal (*Smilacina racemosa*) has red speckled berries, and true Solomon's-seal (*Polygonatum* species) has dark blue berries that dangle from arching stems.

Wild flowers need not be limited to woodlands, especially on small properties where such ideal conditions may be lacking. A few native plants can be grown in the shade of a house wall, under a small tree planted as a terrace or patio decoration, or in the foreground of large shrubs. Nor is it a rule that only native plants be used in a wild-flower garden. There are many introduced plants from other countries that require some shade and so make appropriate companions for the natives.

Two fairly well-known perennials for shade are the primrose and the hosta, the first having beautiful flowers in a variety of forms and colors to brighten spring gardens; the second, more prized for its variegated or textured foliage. Primroses appreciate sunshine during spring — a requirement easily provided in most woodland situations where deciduous (leaf-losing) trees predominate. Later in the summer, the plants receive necessary shade from the fully leaved trees. Hosta plants thrive in varying degrees of shade. A few, such as the nostalgic plantain-lily or August-lily (*Hosta plantaginea*), which has spikes of fragrant white flowers in late summer, are attractive in flower, but generally it is the handsome foliage that makes hosta plants so valued for shade and woodland plantings. A superior hosta is *H. sieboldiana*, which has large, crinkly blue leaves.

Other attractive flowering perennials for woodlands are the various epimediums, which form mounds of neat foliage about 10 inches high. In the spring, epimediums are covered with airy sprays of white, yellow, or ruby flowers which are exceptionally long lasting. Epimediums are fine colonizers, and are attractive in small patches or used as actual ground covers for larger areas.

Daffodils, although not truly shade-loving bulbs, can be naturalized in small or extensive drifts in woodlands, doing especially well in ground exposed to full sunshine in the spring.

Vegetables and the small garden

At first thought, providing space for vegetables on today's generally small properties may seem illogical. For vegetable plants, rarely as decorative (in the landscaping sense, that is) as herbs and other plants, have a reputation for being "bug catchers" and just more trouble than a daily trip to the supermarket's fresh or frozen food department. Of course some vegetable plants and plantings can be messy, and many kinds do take up too much precious space for the value of their harvest. Corn and melon vines are two crops that are hardly suitable for small suburban properties for these reasons. (There is nothing more beautiful than a vast, rolling field of corn, the rows stretching beyond sight, but a few forlorn files of straggly cornstalks hardly beautify the average suburban plot, nor, perhaps even of greater concern, will they provide more than a nibble at the dinner table.)

As for vegetable plants attracting harmful insects and diseases, it is quite true that some do suffer from more than their share. Potato plants, for instance, are susceptible to a number of pests, but few suburban gardeners will want to bother with them anyway. Tomato plants are also pest prone, but the application of an all-purpose vegetable dust or spray (applied as recommended on the can or package) will take care of most problems. (Organic gardeners never use poisonous sprays on their

Bibb lettuce — handsome in the garden, delicious in salads — forms a miniature head, making it desirable for a small vegetable or salad garden. Bibb lettuce, like most other kinds of lettuce, is not difficult to grow, but its seed must be sown in early spring so maximum growth is made during cool weather.

vegetable plants. As suggested in the section on general pest control, page 101, you may decide you can tolerate the bugs on vegetables as readily as you accept them on ornamentals.) And finally, the satisfaction derived from growing some of your own food, the ultimate good eating, and improvement in nutrition are reasons enough for allotting some space to vegetables.

While most recommendations for family vegetable gardens may call for areas 50 by 50 feet or thereabouts, much smaller areas are possible.

136   Landscaping and the Small Garden

And vegetable gardens can be any shape you choose, in addition to the usual square or rectangle. Circular, semicircular, triangular — whatever shapes you have or choose to work with can become a vegetable garden that will be fruitful as well as attractive. In such small gardens, vegetables may be combined with herbs, with the latter providing decorative as well as culinary usage. A small salad garden can include tomato plants (some of the small-fruiting tomato varieties such as 'Tiny Tim,' 'Early Salad,' or 'Small Fry,' are as handsome as they are abundant in harvest); a number of herbs for both decoration and culinary use; lettuce (include some heat-resistant kinds that will withstand summer heat); and a few cucumber vines. To conserve space, the cucumbers might be trained upright on a trellis or vertical strings. The entire garden can be edged with basil or chives.

Tomato plants do not object at all to being grown in pots and other containers on patios or roof gardens, where they provide decoration as well as food. Choose tomato varieties with medium-to-small fruits. Recommended ones are 'Patio,' 'Early Salad,' and 'Small Fry.'

Gardens of Special Plants and for Special Interests 137

If you have neither the space for a salad garden on the order of the one described above nor the space for an old-fashioned garden much larger, there still are ways to enjoy vegetables on today's limited properties. One way is to borrow space from the outdoor living areas, such as a sunny terrace or patio. What could be more convenient than having tubs or long window-box-like wooden planters filled with tomato and cucumber plants and such herbs as basil, chives, tarragon, parsley, and thyme. I have even heard okra recommended for tub or large-pot culture. The okra plant — known as gumbo — is a rather bushy plant, growing about 4 feet high in its dwarf varieties. It has very pretty yellow flowers with red centers which are decidedly ornamental — not so surprising when you know that the okra is a hibiscus and in the same genus as rose-of-Sharon and the tropical shrub rose-of-China. The flowers are followed by the interesting and very nutritious okra pods which are used in soups and shrimp dishes, or simply fried. Okra is an annual which grows fast from seed. (The plants require sunshine and warmth. Usually one plant is allowed to a tub.)

Other vegetables of bush habit, which are decorative as well as prolific with their fruits and therefore are candidates for tub culture, include zucchini, or Italian-type squash, and peppers. (All container-grown vegetables should be planted in rich soil and receive as much sunshine as possible. Because of the limited soil area, more frequent applications of fertilizers are necessary as the plants begin to bear fruit. The concentrated liquid fish fertilizers are excellent for potted plants; follow directions on the package. The tubs or pots should have drainage holes so the soil does not remain waterlogged after rainfall or watering.)

There are still other ways and places in which homeowners can enjoy their own vegetables. Look around your property; no matter how small and crowded it may appear, you are bound to find space for at least a few tomato plants as well as other vegetables. I have a friend who is not otherwise a dedicated gardener but who sows radish seeds every spring around his shrubbery plantings. He acquired this radish-sowing habit as a child, and since then it has been his response to the fever that drives so many of us toward some kind of gardening expression in spring. The radish rows make neat borders, and when the last ones have been harvested, pot-grown seedlings of petunias and impatiens are set in their places — thus ending this man's gardening activity for the year. There is no reason why other vegetables, especially such neat and quick-crop types as lettuce or cress, cannot be handled in a similar fashion on small properties.

A formal garden for vegetables and herbs

Any gardener who has traveled on the byways of Europe, especially in the Mediterranean regions and in Provence, has probably noticed the kitchen gardens that surround homes in both village and country. These gardens, of varying sizes but usually quite compact, can be glimpsed from automobiles, buses, or trains, and are packed tight with salad crops, beans, artichoke plants, and herbs, and are often partially shaded by grape arbors and fruit trees. The memory of these small back-yard (or sometimes front-yard) gardens, and of the more intricate, formal gardens of great estates and public gardens which abound in Europe, provided an idea for one of my most successful vegetable gardens.

It was made in an area about 30 by 35 feet, and was composed of four triangular sections, separated and surrounded by paths about 2½ feet wide. The objective was to plan and plant a vegetable and herb garden that would be attractive to look at and inviting to walk in, yet still yield ingredients for salads as well as beans, squash, and tomatoes in the summer. Chives were planted as a border along the main diagonal path, and a few additional herbs (thyme, oregano, and summer savory) were crowded into an earthenware jar placed in a path intersection off the center of the garden. The jar was ornamental, but with the herbs it contained available for snipping, it served a culinary function as well.

This garden of four parts with rows of spinach, various kinds of lettuce including the Bibb-type varieties, radishes, corn salad, cress, scallions, and roquette (also known as rocket salad) was most attractive during the spring season, but later plantings of beans, squash, and 'Ruby' lettuce (a red-leaved type that is heat-resistant) kept the garden interesting — if not quite as symmetrically neat — and productive during summer.

A small formal or semi-formal garden in similar shapes offers endless variations, and it might well serve as the major garden area on small properties. A mixture of plants could be used, including rows of annuals such as dwarf marigolds or compact varieties of petunias, alternated with a few salad and herb plants, the plant selection and design within the fixed beds changing each year with the whims and needs of the gardener. Or the design could be the basis of an all-green garden, except perhaps for a few color accents in the center such as geraniums. Plants recommended for this purpose include dwarf boxwood, dwarf Japanese holly, teucrium, dwarf barberry, or arctic willow (for very cold climates).

Fruit-yielding gardens

While large fruit gardens are rarely encountered on today's small properties, a certain amount of home-grown fruit can be harvested from smaller gardens. One way to accomplish this is to plant dwarf fruit trees — apple, apricot, peach, pear, and plum. Most grow to only about half the height of standard fruit trees and begin to bear a few years after planting. The fruit on dwarf trees is within easy picking distance, and the trees are much more convenient to spray with average equipment than are standard trees. (Dwarf fruits, alas, fall prey to the same pests that plague the larger trees.)

Certain dwarf forms of peach trees, reaching a height of 3 to 4 feet, are more like peach shrubs. The varieties 'Bonanza,' 'Golden Treasure,' 'Nectarina,' and 'Flory' can be grown in the foreground of shrub borders or in tubs on a terrace. 'Flory' has pretty cerise-colored flowers in spring, rather long, graceful leaves, and an irregular habit of growth that make it quite suitable as an accent in a planting pocket of a terrace or beside steps. The white-fleshed fruits, though rather small, ripen in late fall and are of fairly good eating quality.

Most cherry trees are much too large for small properties, but the varieties 'Meteor,' which eventually reaches 12 to 15 feet, and 'North Star,' which reaches about 8 to 10 feet, are considered semi-dwarf. Homeowners who would like to pick their own cherries and who need a small shade tree will find either of these two varieties most satisfactory. Another small tree, often planted as an ornamental, is the Chinese-date or jujube *(Zizyphus jujuba)*, which yields sweet date-like fruits. It is hardy only in mild climates, where it is attractive near a patio or terrace.

The highbush blueberry is a shrub that is suitable for most small properties, possessing both fruit and an attractive twiggy growth habit, and foliage that turns to bright orange and red in the fall. The bushes can be set out in a row to form an informal hedge or can be placed in landscape groupings, either alone or in combination with other shrubs. Most catalogues offer named varieties that have been selected for their high-quality fruits. Blueberries can be recommended for those with second or summer homes, as the fruits ripen in midsummer. Unlike the raspberry plant, which undeniably produces a most delectable fruit, the blueberry is neat rather than rampant and messy, and requires little care.

A fruit garden for limited space that is as decorative as it is productive. A grapevine has been trained against the side of the building and tubs of the dwarf peach 'Bonanza' stand on gravel beneath the vine.

If you enjoy the rather old-fashioned flavor of stewed rhubarb (try it with sour cream), you will most certainly want to find a place for a few clumps. Usually there is space at the end of even the smallest vegetable plot, but rhubarb is decorative enough to be placed in many situations where its bold foliage makes a handsome accent.

Pools and water gardens

Water gardens can be excellent features for small gardens. Pools can be constructed to fit a variety of situations, and to be appealing do not have to be large or complicated. A small pool can be built in one end of a patio. A small tree or shrub or group of small shrubs and a few

A shallow, saucer-shaped pool has been lined with various sizes of pebbles and round stones which extend beyond the edge of the pool. A small fountain is maintained by a pump which recirculates the water. The stones were merely scattered artfully over the bottom of the pool. The pool is shallow enough to require no forms in its construction.

potted plants can be added. If the pool is deep enough, there are pygmy varieties of water-lilies, which can be planted for color and evening scent. Or you can build or improvise very shallow pools — mere scoops in the earth — for small reflecting pools, which also invite birds. These shallow pools can be made of concrete and do not require complicated reinforcements because their sides are sloping. Premolded Fiberglas pools in various shapes and sizes can be obtained from nurseries and water-garden specialists, but they often look artificial and garish — just like the plastic objects they are — unless they are carefully

142 Landscaping and the Small Garden

integrated with their surroundings by skillful use of rocks and plants.

Very temporary pools can be made by presenting plastic sheeting into a depression in the earth. As with the premolded pools, some effort must be made to conceal the edges, but if you are not sure you want a permanent garden pool, a plastic-lined pool is a worth-while experiment.

Gardens of roses

Roses remain among the most popular of all flowering shrubs, despite the fact that today few homeowners have the space or will to devote to growing more than a few varieties. But those few varieties can add a tremendous amount of color to the property in early summer, and most homeowners have more space for roses than they realize. One idea worth copying was carried out by a neighbor who made a border of hybrid tea and floribunda roses on the inside of a split-rail fence that ran across the front of his lot. It was an informal border, quite in harmony with his modified Colonial house and the fence, with usually three of one variety of rose grouped together. Large-flowered purple clematis vines were planted and trained against the posts, making a startling and welcome color contrast to the various pinks, reds, and white of the rose blooms. More traditional — and always effective — are climber or rambler roses trained along a split-rail fence.

Floribunda roses will thrive for at least a season in tubs or large pots on sunny terraces. More permanence from roses results when planting them as a border along one side of a terrace. The old pink-flowered variety known as 'The Fairy' is especially recommended for this purpose, as it is nearly everblooming. Although it is not completely pest free, it is far less susceptible to most rose ills than are the majority of roses. It lacks fragrance, and in midsummer and in very hot weather the flowers tend to fade, but still and all, this is a fine rose for those who want durability and a long season of bloom without fuss.

In very small gardens, there is a fine opportunity to experiment with miniature roses. These little bushes grow from 8 to 15 inches tall, depending on the variety, and have foliage and flowers that remain in suitable proportion and harmony to the size of the plant. The effectiveness of miniature roses can be lost on large properties unless they are used properly, but in small gardens and small patios and terraces they can be charming. They are ideal in any kind of container, and are

Gardens of Special Plants and for Special Interests 143

especially appropriate in boxes placed on terrace walls where they can be appreciated at eye level. Miniature roses can be grouped (use at least three of each variety) in the foreground of flower gardens, or they can be set out to serve as a low hedge or edging. In fact, roses of every size and kind can be freely mixed with other flowering plants. In a flower garden of annuals and perennials, one or more tree roses can be set at suitable intervals (according to the length of the border) as dramatic color accents. Floribunda and hybrid tea-rose plants can be used among other flowering plants in the same fashion. Consider also the use of climber roses against posts or trellises as background in a mixed flower garden.

Roses are marvelously adaptable to patio and terrace areas. Rose-trellises can be arranged in a series along a side of the terrace, providing privacy and protection as well as beauty. The pillar or climber roses that grow against the trellises will thrive so long as they have sun and well-drained soil. Fragrance is also supplied when you select such scented beauties as 'Climbing Etoile de Hollande,' 'Climbing Chrysler,' 'Climbing Talisman,' or 'Climbing Sutter's Gold.' A tree rose can be an elegant feature on the terrace when planted in a tub. Or use two trees — one at each side of the steps leading to the lawn. A border of hybrid teas or floribunda roses can decorate the edges of the patio.

Winter garden effects

In mild climates, garden appreciation and activity can continue nearly all year. January in many southern areas means the beginning of the camellia and azalea season, but in a large part of this country, January's wintry weather causes most people to assume that any interest in the outdoor garden is ludicrous. Yet there are good reasons for considering how your garden looks in winter and what plants you might add to make these bleak months more pleasurable for you and your family. One reason is the welcome trend to take maximum advantage of a property's existing features when designing and locating the house, a trend that increases awareness of the outdoors and elements in all seasons of the year. There is also the fact that more and more we tend to live in glass houses with even the most economical dwellings showing larger windows or entire wall sections of sliding glass doors, thus increasing the integration between interiors and surrounding landscape.

Seasons in the garden: In spring, the early flowering heaths (Erica carnea) *bloom over a period of many weeks. The woodland beyond is filled with color from daffodils and an especially early-flowering rhododendron hybrid appropriately called 'Vernus.'*

And finally you will discover that the winter aspect of many plants, both as individuals or when viewed in combination with other kinds of plants, offers much of interest in form, silhouette, texture, or structure quite different from other seasons. Some effects can be admired from a distance, but other special winter characteristics are details to be appreciated under closer scrutiny. Few gardeners today have the keen interest or even the available necessary space to plan winter gardens or walk-along borders in which all plant material is selected and arranged solely for its appeal in the winter season (although this used to be accepted practice on estates and large properties), but even small gardens can contain some plantings of winter interest.

The most obviously important plants in the winter landscape are coniferous evergreens — pines, spruces, firs, and others — which in summer tend to blend with the surrounding greenery but in winter months can be dominant features. They also emphasize the winter outline,

Seasons in the garden: In summer, pink, rose, lavender, and white flower color is provided by the heath and heather garden above the stone retaining wall. The woodland beyond becomes a retreat of shade and shadow forms.

bark colors and textures, and structure of leaf-losing trees and shrubs, which can be starkly beautiful without their foliage.

There are conifers for every region and quite a few which thrive in most parts of the country, but you will want to consult a local nurseryman for recommendations suitable to your area.

While available space for many conifers is limited in small gardens, there is usually ample space for dwarf coniferous evergreens, which may be miniature replicas of standard evergreens or differ quite radically in habit and characteristics. Most possess in common, though, true dwarfness, and may remain only a few feet in height and width for many, many years. These dwarf evergreens are appealing in any season, but in winter their exceptional characteristics — unique forms and color and texture of foliage — are more evident, whatever their setting, such as in a small rock garden or standing alone surrounded by snow. There are dwarfs among the firs, spruces, hemlocks, and many other conifers.

Seasons in the garden: A late winter snow storm frosts the heath and heather garden in the foreground and the azaleas, rhododendrons and other plants in the woodland.

Dwarf forms of the common hemlock *(Tsuga canadensis)* are often much more suitable for small gardens than are the eventually large-growing parents. Several named forms of dwarf hemlock are available from specialists who deal in rock-garden plants.

An American or English holly tree, its branches strung with bright red berries and standing as a proud sentinel on snow-covered ground, can be "winter garden" enough for many homeowners, especially when it is placed within viewing distance from a picture window or through glass sliding doors from a living room. Hollies, as accents or in mingling groups, become elegant landscape features for all seasons. (Remember you must have a male holly somewhere on your property or your neighbor's to ensure pollination of the female's flowers in spring, as only female plants are berry bearers.)

Gardens of Special Plants and for Special Interests 147

The American or English hollies are the most familiar tree forms of the genus, but there are many other hollies, mostly with evergreen foliage (not always prickly or sharp pointed) and of more shrubby habit. One is the Japanese holly (*Ilex crenata*), a shrub with dense, glistening foliage and an attractive habit especially noticeable in winter. It has many varieties, some of which are very dwarf and resemble boxwood.

Another outstanding shrub for its large, winter-long red berries is the broad-leaved evergreen shrub skimmia *(Skimmia japonica)*. As with American and English hollies, it is the female skimmia which bears the berries, but the male plant offers clusters of small, yet intensely fragrant flowers in early spring. Skimmia is a low-growing but wide-spreading plant, remaining at about 4 feet or so in height. Unfortunately, it is not hardy in those northern areas where winter temperatures hover around zero for extended periods, but it is perfectly winter hardy on Long Island, New York, and in similar areas. In such northern regions, most broad-leaved evergreens — rhododendrons, azaleas, andromeda, and others — must be omitted from the landscape in favor of the more rugged conifers, junipers, and yews. Among the last two are many fine subjects, both in tree and shrub forms, and, in the case of junipers, possessing handsome needle colors and textures.

What about flowers in the snow? The notion is not quite the fairy tale it may seem, and many people have heard of the Christmas-rose, which, undaunted by snow or cold, produces pure-white flowers, somewhat reminiscent of a single rose, all winter from November to March. The plants, which have evergreen foliage, grow about 15 inches high and are fine subjects in woodlands among wild flowers or in the foreground of shrub borders where they receive some summer shade. The flowers will lift the spirits of the most winter-weary soul or provide good reason for the skeptical to visit the garden in winter.

The witch-hazels, both the natives and the imported species from the Orient, are indomitable winter-blooming shrubs, the flowers opening during warm spells from January into early spring. The flowers, odd but much appreciated in winter, possess wispy yellow petals that curl into balls in very cold weather but quickly unfurl as the temperature moderates, a characteristic that gives the flowers longevity and durability throughout the most trying of winters.

Other reliable winter flowers are found among the heaths *(Erica)*, low-growing shrubs with tiny, needle-like foliage which is evergreen. The flowers, little bells in white, magenta, or rose, seem to last forever.

A fresh covering of snow enhances the winter beauty of a heath (Erica), a low-growing evergreen shrub. Winter brings out the beauty of many plants which tend to be less conspicuous in other seasons. Bark patterns, leaf textures, branch arrangement, even leaf and flower buds become especially prominent during the winter months.

Their buds form in the fall, begin to show color as winter approaches, and are a conspicuous part of the plant. Some flower sprays will be fully developed by Christmas, and thereafter more flowers will appear until the blooming peak — late winter to early spring — is reached. The heaths require light, acid soil (a predominantly sandy soil to which peat moss is added at planting time is good), and full sun. Although the plants can be injured in very cold winters, they are worth the gamble for their cheering flowers. The most reliable heaths are 'King George,' 'Springwood White,' 'Springwood Pink,' and 'Darleyensis.'

Many other winter effects, such as the tiered-branch arrangement and twiggy growth terminated by prominent flower buds of the flowering dogwood or the large, furry flower buds of the star magnolia, come from plants chosen because of their value in the landscape in the green months. And there are many other commonly used trees and shrubs that can contribute dramatic beauty to winter. Some of this beauty will depend on how and where the plants are placed, but much of it can come solely from the plants themselves. Even the ubiquitous forsythia takes on a different character in winter as its numerous flower buds begin to swell against yellowish-brown bark.

A list of plants to consider for effectiveness in winter

EVERGREEN TREES FOR MANY REGIONS

American arborvitae (*Thuja occidentalis*)
Colorado spruce (*Picea pungens*)
Colorado white fir (*Abies concolor*)
Common hemlock (*Tsuga canadensis*)
Common spruce (*Picea abies*)
*Deodar cedar (*Cedrus deodara*)
Douglas-fir (*Pseudotsuga menziesii*)
English yew (*Taxus baccata*)
Hinoki-cypress (*Chamaecyparis obtusa*)
**Holly (*Ilex aquifolium* and *I. opaca*)
Japanese yew (*Taxus cuspidata*)
Juniper (*Juniperus* — many good ones)
Oriental arborvitae (*Thuja orientalis*)
Pine (*Pinus* — many kinds)
Umbrella-pine (*Sciadopitys verticillata*)

* Not reliably hardy far north.
** Not for Southwest, Rocky Mountains, or Plains areas.

DWARF EVERGREENS

Birdsnest spruce (*Picea abies* 'Nidiformis')
Dwarf Alberta spruce (*Picea glauca* 'Conica')
Dwarf balsam fir (*Abies balsamea hudsonia*)
Dwarf columnar juniper (*Juniperus communis* 'Compressa')
Dwarf hemlock (*Tsuga canadensis* 'Hussii')
Dwarf Japanese juniper (*Juniperus procumbens* 'Nana')
Dwarf Japanese yew (*Taxus cuspidata nana*)
Dwarf white pine (*Pinus strobus* 'Nana')
*Edging box (*Buxus sempervirens* 'Suffruticosa')
False-cypress (*Chamaecyparis* — many dwarf forms)
Heller Japanese holly (*Ilex crenata* 'Helleri')
Kingswood dwarf box (*Buxus microphylla* 'Compacta')
Korean box (*Buxus microphylla koreana*)
Mugho pine (*Pinus mugo*)

* Not reliably hardy far north.

This front-entrance city garden which can be enjoyed by passers-by as well as residents of the town house is certainly an example of a special problem handled well. The soil for the garden is enclosed by a gracefully curved wall of broken flagstone pieces. The plants in such a garden can be changed from season to season. Potted hyacinths and daffodils can be set out in spring; then as they fade, can be whisked away to make room for geraniums, marigolds, and other summer-flowering plants, with chrysanthemums added for fall color.

7 Small Garden Ideas and Plant Combinations

Accent Planting for Terrace — Three or more daffodil bulbs (plant in fall) with a few clumps of the evergreen creeping *Sedum acre,* which has yellow flowers in late spring. Other creeping sedums can be used. If terrace has jigsaw paving of flagstones or other flat rocks, remove two or three stones to make a planting area, preferably toward side away from traffic, although a stray footstep or two will not harm sedums unduly. This is a cheerful arrangement for early spring, especially pleasant to view from inside the house.

Partially Shaded Bay Formed by Shrubs — 2 or 3 yellow-flowering day-lilies, 2 or 3 blue-flowering hosta plants, and foreground edging of white-flowered wax begonia plants. (Number of plants depends on available space.)

Tree-shrub Grouping for Diagonal Corner from House Front or at Property Corner — Flowering dogwood tree (or white birch, or vase-shaped flowering crabapple) and 2 or 3 evergreen azalea shrubs (or low-spreading junipers or yews or mugho pines) and ground cover of myrtle (*Vinca minor*). A few clumps of tulips or daffodils can be planted in the fall for color accent in spring.

Small Flower Garden for Midsummer Effect — Could be in back-yard corner, or in front of shrubs along boundary. Wherever used, a background of shrubs, evergreens, fence, or wall enhances the effect. Three to 5 tall yellow day-lilies (select midsummer varieties), 1 or 2 plants of

152 Landscaping and the Small Garden

babys-breath, about 5 to 6 plants of blue-flowering *Nepeta mussinii* (a kind of catmint with blue-green foliage) or ageratum, and a final edging of a yellow French marigold.

Coniferous Evergreen Grouping for Year-round Greenery — Pyramidal arborvitae (1), 3 Pfitzer junipers, 5 mugho pines. An elegant grouping ideal for snow-country dwellers as an "island" in the lawn or near the terrace where it can be viewed from indoors.

Pink and Blue Doorway Garden — Pink flowering almond shrubs (1 to 5 depending on available space), about 50 blue grape-hyacinth bulbs (plant in fall) for spring color. Continue pink-and-blue color scheme through summer with pink petunia and blue lobelia plants.

Raised Bed or Planter Combination for Patio or Entry — Red geraniums, mixed-color Thumbelina zinnias, and white petunias. The petunias will tumble over the sides of the planter.

Temporary Hedge or Screen to Grow from Seed — Castor bean (5 to 8 feet) makes a lush, effective screen. For additional display, plant seeds of spiderflower (*Cleome*) and tall African marigolds in front. Another annual, kochia (sometimes called summer-cypress), can be grown from seed to make a 30-inch formal hedge along the outer edge of a patio.

Wild Flowers and Perennial Plants for Small Shade Garden — 3 to 5 ferns (any tall kind such as marginal shield fern, Christmas fern, royal, etc.), 5 white hesperis (sweet rocket), 3 plantain-lily (also called August-lily), 5 epimedium, and 8 to 12 primroses. This garden will require rich humus soil. Add peat moss, mixing it thoroughly with the soil before planting.

Three Perennials for Midsummer Color — Redhot poker plant (*Kniphofia*); day-lily (*Hemerocallis*); and globe-thistle (*Echinops*). The color scheme is flamboyant (orange-red and yellow or creamy yellow from the red-hot poker; yellow, orange or rust from the day-lily; and steely blue from the globe-thistle) and the flower effect, exotic. Group these perennials against a large boulder or against shrubs, or combine with other flowering plants (zinnia, marigold, phlox).

Small Garden Ideas and Plant Combinations 153

Color and Texture for Partial Shade — Tuberous begonias (not for *dense* shade) ferns, such as lady fern (*Athyrium filix-femina*) or marginal wood fern (*Dryopteris marginalis*); and hosta.

Dwarf Evergreens as Terrace Accents — There are many kinds — fascinating because of unique needle texture and plant form. Many may remain for years within a few feet of the same height and width. Use them in wooden tubs or insert an occasional plant, such as a mugho pine, in an "island" left open within a brick-covered terrace. The plants will be large enough so guests won't trample on them.

Boundary Planting for Beauty and Privacy — If you have an especially wide lot, plant a mixture of large deciduous shrubs with a generous intermingling of pyramidal evergreens, such as arborvitae (*Thuja*); red-cedar juniper (*Juniperus virginiana*); western red-cedar (*Juniperus scopulorum*); and other evergreens available in your region. The evergreens will add a touch of formality and be of great value in winter when the deciduous shrubs are bare of leaves.

White and Green for Spring — Under and around a white flowering dogwood tree, plant several clumps of foamflower (*Tiarella cordifolia*), a native perennial plant that has spires of white flowers. The dogwood and foam-flower bloom together in spring. A few Christmas ferns can be included among the foam-flower clumps, the foliage of both covering the ground after the spring season. Foam-flower needs partial shade and humus-rich soil.

Picture for Winter — The bright yellow flower petals of the Chinese witch-hazel (*Hamamelis mollis*) against a clear blue sky from midwinter to early spring. The presence of snow adds to the contrast.

Small Formal Rose Garden — An elegant touch to a formal terrace. Take a formal shape — rectangular or octagonal — and make it into a rose garden adjacent to or incorporated within the terrace. A rectangle or octagon, about 6 feet wide and 8 feet long, will accommodate two tree roses, one at each end, and a block of four floribunda roses in between. (Space the floribunda roses about 24 inches or so apart.) Surround the garden with white-flowered sweet-alyssum (easy from seed). Mulch the surface with a *coarse* grade of peat moss (poultry grade) or pine-bark

Evergreens grown in bonsai style, such as this specimen, are decorative when displayed occasionally on a terrace or in a lath shelter, as here. The tabletop has been made from a large pebble-surfaced concrete slab. A lath house can be a pleasant retreat from sun and wind for people as well as for such plants as orchids, ferns, and fuchsias. As can be seen from a comparison of this and the preceding picture, the range of containers runs the gamut.

mulch. For a very formal effect, mulch with white marble chips, substituting a dwarf yellow French marigold or lavender sweet-alyssum for the white variety suggested above.

Winter Embellishment for a Wall or Fence — The hardy-orange, also called trifoliate-orange (*Poncirus trifoliata*), has thorny green twigs, fascinating to look at, especially in its leafless winter attire. On older plants, small "oranges" are attractive during fall season.

Bench Surrounded by Fragrance — In the bay formed by a mixed shrubbery planting, place a bench. At each end of the bench plant a very fragrant shrub accent — such as Burkwood viburnum (*Viburnum burkwoodii*), Carlesi viburnum (*V. carlesii*), or a fragrant mock-orange. For spring, summer, and fall fragrance, consider the sweetbrier rose (*Rosa eglanteria*), which has delightfully fruit-scented foliage and pretty pink flowers in early summer. Like many shrub roses, the sweetbrier is vigorous and must have its long shoots cut back in early spring to keep it compact enough for small properties.

Star Magnolia with Spring Bulbs — Surround the ground just under and around the reach of the outer branches with a thick planting of the little spring bulbs: snowdrops, grape-hyacinths, crocuses, glory-of-the-snow, scilla, and puschkinia. For a fine, yet careless, color effect, scatter the bulbs; or for a patchwork-quilt effect, plant the bulbs in blocks. Some will bloom before the star magnolia's beautiful white flowers open, others at the same time.

Gray and Yellow Border — A subtle, sophisticated combination, simple to achieve with a variety of plants and useful in planters, along walks and drives, as borders to patio or terrace, or in terrace "island." For the gray, use such foliage plants as dusty miller (very popular on the West Coast and readily available elsewhere from garden centers), santolina (an aromatic shrubby plant often grown in herb gardens and widely available from garden centers and mail-order nurseries), succulents such as echeveria (for West Coast and mild climates), blue arctic willow (very hardy), catmint (*Nepeta mussini*), or Silver Mound artemisia. For yellow, use dwarf French marigold (can be grown from seed), or buy yellow chrysanthemum plants.

Peter Pan zinnia has coral-pink or plum-colored flowers on stocky, well-branched plants which do not exceed a foot in height. It is an outstanding annual to grow in the foreground of shrubs, such as its use here in front of a low yew hedge, or as a border around a terrace or patio.

Shrubs Under Low Window — Two golden-leaved mock-orange (4 feet) or two golden privet (4 feet) and twelve blue arctic willows trimmed as hedge about 2½ feet high. Place one yellow-leaved shrub at each end of willow hedge. A fine combination for ranch-type houses with low or picture windows in colder northern areas.

Small Perennial Garden for Autumn Color — Three blue monkshood, five yellow chrysanthemums, seven low-growing hardy asters (white or pink), three or four clumps of blue-flowered plumbago (*Ceratostigma plumbaginoides*).

Shrub Planting Around Lampost — Two or three Andorra juniper (or other low-growing juniper) and four to five 'Gold Drop' potentilla. The junipers provide all-season greenery; the potentilla shrubs (about 2 feet high) provide bright yellow flowers all summer.

Succession of White for Terrace or Roof Garden — A generous use of white — in furniture, pot and container color, and in the plants themselves — white geraniums, white sweet-alyssum, white-and-green-leaved caladium, white pansies, white Peruvian-daffodils, white snapdragons, and white petunias.

Fun with formality was the idea behind the creation of this brick-surfaced terrace, especially intriguing when viewed from an adjacent deck or the upper floors of a town house. While its pleasing design and proportions show careful planning, its execution and maintenance are not as complicated as might be thought. Curved or circular lines have been eliminated in favor of straight, angular forms, making the brickwork much easier. Geraniums provide color within the beds outlined by boxwood.

158 Landscaping and the Small Garden

Terrace Color for Early Fall — In a terrace planting pocket or "hole," set two or three plumbago (*Ceratostigma plumbaginoides*) plants, the number of plants being determined by the size of the "hole." (Plumbago is a low, spreading, shrub-like plant that behaves more like a perennial in most northern areas. It grows about 1 foot high and slowly spreads.) A few squat pots of yellow or white chrysanthemums can be placed nearby to contrast with the bright blue flowers of plumbago, which appear in late summer and last into early fall. The foliage of plumbago has a bronze cast and is attractive in the period before flowers appear.

Spring Garden with Wisteria — Plant a tree wisteria in the corner of a property, or near a terrace or patio. Plant tulips in shades of lilac, lavender, or purple in front and under the wisteria; or choose contrasting colors among the tulips, such as pink or yellow or white. Among the tulips, set out pansies. (When tulips and pansies have finished blooming, plant annuals such as petunia and sweet-alyssum.)

Against a Chimney — Many modern dwellings have huge outdoor chimney expanses for their lavish indoor fireplaces. Plant a single pyracantha (*Pyracantha coccinea*) against the chimney, pruning as necessary to keep its habit espaliered and contained. Complement the pyracantha's fall berry display with several plants of chrysanthemums, also in harvest colors, such as yellow, rust, or maroon, moved into position when the berries turn orange.

Planting a Brick-paved Terrace — Outline the terrace with a wide (about 3 feet or so) border of English ivy (*Hedera helix baltica*) or periwinkle (*Vinca minor*). Ask your nurseryman to help you select one multi-stemmed tree (white birch and Chinese elm are examples) and place it at one end of terrace within English ivy (border can be widened around base of tree). To balance the tree asymmetrically, select two slow-growing coniferous evergreens (two yews — even the narrow Irish yew might be appropriate — or two upright junipers such as the Swedish juniper; or dwarf arborvitae, either rounded or conical in shape), to place at the opposite sides of the terrace. This arrangement works best with a free-form terrace. Try the plan on paper first!

Colorful Threesome for Midsummer — One vitex, three to four 'Bluebird' rose-of-Sharon, and twenty-four dwarf yellow French marigolds. The vitex, a large shrub with spikes of lovely lavender-blue flowers, begins to bloom in midsummer, with blooms lasting into fall. 'Bluebird' rose-of-Sharon, about 3 to 4 feet tall, begins to flower in early summer. A fine grouping for the vacation home.

Summer Color for Shade in Front of Camellias or Rhododendrons — White-leaved caladiums, tuberous begonias, a dozen or so white- or pink-flowered wax begonias.

Around Trunk of Large Shade Tree — Three to four ferns, three to four hosta plants, periwinkle as ground cover. A few daffodil bulbs could be planted for early spring color and to contrast with blue flowers of periwinkle.

Carpet of Color in Geometric Patterns — An idea borrowed from the artist Mondrian! Employ low-growing, almost ground-hugging varieties of annuals, and plant them in blocks of one color, close together so that flowers will hide foliage and give continuous color effect. Good ones include: white sweet-alyssum; mini-pink Thumbelina dwarf zinnia; ageratum; lobelia; extra dwarf impatiens varieties; dwarf marigold; and miniature petunia varieties (6 to 8 inches). Use a good seed catalogue (George W. Park Seed Company, Greenwood, South Carolina 29646) for planning help and as a source for seeds; or buy your plants from a local outlet. Blocks of colored gravel give additional interest.

Hardy Broad-leaved Evergreens for Foundation Accent — Two to three 'Sarcoxie' euonymus (4 feet, but readily pruned to lower heights); one to two Korean boxwood (2 to 4 feet). In very cold climates, some protection from bright winter sun is essential to prevent foliage from browning. However, injured foliage is readily cut off in spring.

Foundation Accent for Shade — Skimmia (*Skimmia japonica*) and ground-cover planting of sweet woodruff (*Asperula*). Skimmia is a broad-leaved evergreen for mild climates and protected sections of the garden and around the house in climates similar to that of Long Island and New York City.

Flowering Shrub Border for Colorful Spring — For a wide lot, plant an informal hedge of different kinds of flowering shrubs. Include the following: forsythia, Sargent crabapple, hawthorn, spirea, virburnum, and shrub forms of honeysuckle. Make informal plantings of spring-flowering

160   Landscaping and the Small Garden

bulbs in front — daffodils, tulips, hyacinths, scilla, glory-of-the-snow. Make this your spring garden if you go away in the summer.

Tawny Colors to Complement Wooden Siding or Shingles of House — Or the brick of a wall or chimney. Use spirit-lifting colors — orange, yellow, brown and red — easily found in such annuals as French marigold, annual gaillardia, Persian carpet zinnia, creeping-zinnia (*Sanvitalia procumbens*) and others.

June Splendor from Bearded Iris — The bearded iris is one of the perennials that seem to fit into any number of landscape situations. Modern varieties are spectacularly beautiful and possess an intoxicating perfume most appropriate for early summer. If you go away in July and August, plant one side of a terrace with a double or triple row. The plants are tough enough to survive neglect during your absence (lack of water, control of weeds) and of course will have flowered before your departure. Other areas for a few — or several — iris clumps: in a bay formed by shrubs, providing the area is nearly sunny all day; along house or garage wall; or in an irregularly shaped "island" in lawn, a rather old-fashioned practice back in style. Don't waste garden space on out-of-date iris varieties — few are worth it. New varieties are superior in every way and are never very expensive. (Iris can be divided every third year or so.)

Miniature Herb Garden for Terrace Table or Wall — Take a squat pot or any container with a diameter of about 8 to 12 inches (an old earthenware casserole or other kitchen castoff may be just right), fill it with soil and several divisions of herb plants. Or visit your local greenhouse and buy plants in 2¼-inch pots. Either way the plants will be crowded, yet will display varying characteristics in foliage and aroma as they supply snippings for the cook. The pot can stand on a low table or wall in the outdoor living area for all to enjoy.

Living Sculpture All Winter — Take one shrub, the compact form of winged euonymus or spindle tree (*Euonymus alatus* 'Compactus'), and place it where you can enjoy its unique winter pattern — near an entrance, in a tub on a paved area adjacent to house window or glassed area, as an accent at the start of a frequently used walk. You will find that you will never tire of observing the frame of this small shrub (eventual height may be 4 to 5 feet but regular pruning will keep it lower) with its slightly arching branches embellished with cork encrustations. You can use your pruners — as a sculptor would his tools — to shape the shrub into a pleasing form. Another plus from this shrub is its brilliant autumn foliage, the reason why it is also known as "burning bush."

Perennial Combination for Early Summer — Pink astilbe, several clumps of sweet William (*Dianthus barbatus*) in mixed colors (the various shades of reds, pinks, rose, and white, usually in bicolor combinations, are as royal and rich as the colors in an Oriental carpet), and the hardy geranium known as 'Johnson's Blue.'

A Large Shrub Border — For boundary or screen planting for the larger lot. Forsythia, mock-orange (*Philadelphus*), Cornelian-cherry (*Cornus mas*), sweetbrier rose (*Rosa eglanteria*), and butterfly-bush (*Buddleia davidii*). The number of plants of each kind of shrub selected depends on the size of the property. Probably fewer shrubs of forsythia and more of mock-orange may be more appealing; select different varieties of mock-orange or both single or double flowered varieties, but be sure all are fragrant! The sweetbrier rose has single pink flowers that will bloom with the mock-orange and apple- or pineapple-scented foliage. Butterfly-bush possesses the one virtue of giving quite showy flowers in summer. Rose-of-Sharon could be added as companion plants-in-flower to the butterfly-bush.

Cacti and Succulents in Containers — An easy maintenance idea for homeowners in the West, Midwest, and East. The containers can be large squat pots, troughs, or wooden planters, or whatever fits into the terrace or patio scheme. Use one kind of plant or combinations of different ones for varying foliage colors, forms and textures. Many will flower in summer. Sun is needed and overwatering can be fatal.

Large Shrubs into Small Trees — Many large shrubs, by training and simple pruning, can be transformed into small tree-like plants, sometimes with multiple trunks, thereby becoming more suitable in scale to small gardens or crowded areas of larger gardens. One such shrub is red-vein enkianthus (*Enkianthus campanulatus*), which has an attractive gray-barked trunk. Another is the native spice-bush (*Lindera benzoin*).

Gray and Pink for Early Summer — For weeks of effective color and contrast in form and texture, combine the salmon-flowered 'Newport Pink'

Many containers today are nearly as much sculpture as they are receptacles for various kinds of plants. The sculptural quality of this large concrete bowl is echoed by the formalized, waxen-appearing succulents. This planter in a public mall is too large a decoration for most home grounds, but homeowners can adapt from it on a more suitable scale. Shopping malls and other public areas are often full of ideas for home landscaping.

sweet William with drifts of the velvet-textured and gray-leaved lamb's-ears (*Stachys olympica*). A substitute for the salmon-colored sweet William would be petunias or one of the small-flowered, low-growing zinnia varieties such as 'Peter Pan Pink,' Thumbelina 'Mini-pink' or 'Mini-coral.' Lamb's-ears is an easy-to-grow, spreading perennial for sun or semi-shade and is attractive all summer.

Small Garden Ideas and Plant Combinations   163

Blue Companions for Yellow Day-lilies — A summer perennial garden for a corner of the property or for a garden just off one side of a terrace could contain six yellow day-lilies (more or less in number, according to available space), two globe-thistles (*Echinops*), and three sea-holly (*Eryngium*). These are all large, bushy perennials that possess no cultural quirks — unlike the more refined, always dramatic blue delphinium.

Late Spring Shrub Twosome — Any large-flowered purple lilac (*Syringa*) and in the foreground the variegated green-and-white foliaged selection of the single yellow-flowered shrub, *Kerria japonica*. The single kerria is much more attractive than the commonly planted double-flowered form, and is more compact in growth, too, reaching about 4 feet.

Early Summer Shrub Twosome as Ground Cover — For sunny slopes or flat ground with acid, humusy soil, combine the heath 'C. D. Eason' (a form of *Erica cinerea*), which grows from 6 to 8 inches high and has glowing rosy red flowers of neon intensity, with the Japanese alpine spirea (*Spiraea bumalda alpina*), which has pale rose-pinkish flower clusters on broadly spreading plants about 1 foot high. Both remain in bloom for several weeks.

SUGGESTED BOOKS FOR FURTHER REFERENCE

GENERAL

America's Garden Book, Louise and James Bush-Brown. Charles Scribner's Sons. Revised 1965.

The Complete Book of Garden Magic, Roy E. Biles. Completely revised and edited by Marjorie J. Dietz. J. G. Ferguson Publishing Company. 1969.

TREES AND SHRUBS

The Concise Encyclopedia of Favorite Flowering Shrubs, Marjorie J. Dietz. Doubleday & Company. 1963.

Evergreens for Every State, Katherine M. P. Cloud. Chilton Company. 1960.

Flowering Shrubs, Isabel Zucker. D. Van Nostrand Company. 1966.

Handbook on Conifers. A handbook of the Brooklyn Botanic Garden. 1969.

Shrubs and Trees for the Home Landscape, James Bush-Brown. Chilton Company. 1963.

Shrubs and Trees for the Small Place, P. J. Van Melle. Revised by Montague Free. Doubleday & Company. 1955.

Shrubs and Vines for American Gardens, Donald Wyman. The Macmillan Company. Revised 1969.

1200 Trees and Shrubs — Where to Buy Them. A handbook of the Brooklyn Botanic Garden. 1970.

SPECIAL PLANTS AND SUBJECTS

Anyone Can Grow Roses, Cynthia Westcott. D. Van Nostrand. 1960.

Bulbs for Summer Bloom, John Phillip Baumgardt. Hawthorn Books. 1970.

The Complete Book of Bulbs, F. F. Rockwell and Esther C. Grayson. Doubleday & Company. 1953.

The Complete Book of Growing Plants from Seed, Elda Haring. Diversity Books. 1967.

The Concise Encyclopedia of Favorite Wild Flowers, Marjorie J. Dietz. Doubleday & Company. 1965.

Container Gardening, Indoors and Out, Jack Kramer. Doubleday & Company. 1970.

The Fragrant Year, Helen Van Pelt Wilson and Leonie Bell. M. Barrows & Company. 1967.

A Garden of Herbs, Eleanour Sinclair Rohde. Soft-cover reprint by Dover Publications. 1970.

The Home Garden Cookbook: From Seed to Plate, Ken and Pat Kraft. Doubleday & Company. 1969.

Rhododendrons of the World, David Leach. Charles Scribner's Sons. 1961.

Rock Gardening, H. Lincoln Foster. Houghton Mifflin Company. 1968.

Summer Flowers for Continuing Bloom. A handbook of the Brooklyn Botanic Garden. 1968.

Index

Abelia, 46, 61
Acanthus, 87
Acer. *See* Maple
Achimenes, 124
Adiantum, 133
Aegopodium, 33
Agapanthus, 87
Ageratum, 108, *110*, 115, 152, 159
Agricultural extension service, 19
Ailanthus, 45, 93
Ajuga, 22, 32, 93, 124
Akebia, 67
Albizzia. *See* Silk-tree
Allium, 120
Almond, flowering, 152
Alyssum. *See* Basket-of-gold; Sweet-alyssum
Amelanchier, 44, *129*
Amur cork-tree, 38, 39
Andromeda, 51, 124
Annuals, 108, 115-17, 159, 160
Antirrhinum. *See* Snapdragon
Aphids, 103
Apple, dwarf, 139
Apricot, dwarf, 139
Aquilegia, 133
Araucaria, 90
Arborvitae, 59, 61, 86, 152, 153, 158
Archangel, 33
Arctostaphylos, 32
Artemisia, 155
Ash, flowering, 41. *See also* Mountain-ash
Asiatic beetle, 104
Asperula, 159
Aster, 156
Astilbe, 161
Athyrium, 153
Aucuba, 89
August-lily, 133
Avocado, 86
Azalea, *5*, 9, 46, 52, 54, 86, 94, 124, 132, *146*, 151

Babys-breath, 105, 122, 152
Bacterial control, 104
Barberry, 48-49, 61
Barrenwort, 32, 152
Basil, 125, 126, 128
Basket-of-gold, 106, 118
Bauhinia, 43
Bearberry, 32
Bear's-breech, 87
Begonia. *See* Tuberous-rooted begonia; Wax begonia
Berberis. *See* Barberry
Bergenia, 124
Bermuda grass, 24
Betula. *See* Birch

Bibb lettuce, *135*
Birch, 38, 39, 40, 41, 74, 83, 151, 158
Black haw, 39
Bleeding heart, 105, 109, 111, 118
Bluebell. *See* Scilla
Blueberry, 139
Blue fescue, 32
Bluegrass, 24
Boston-ivy, 66
Boxwood, 48, 61, 72, 74, 87, 124, *157*, 159
Broad-leaved evergreens, 46-51, 147, 159
Buckthorn, 61
Buckwheat hull mulch, 100
Buddleia, 161
Bugleweed, 32
Bulbs, 93, 114, 117-24, 155
Burning bush, 161
Butterfly-bush, 161
Buxus. *See* Boxwood

Cacti, *8*, 161
Caladium, 32, 87, 124, 157, 159
Calluna. *See* Heather
Camellia, 46, 49, 86, 87, *94*, 124, 159
Cankerworms, 101
Cardinal-flower, 133
Castor bean, 152
Catalpa, 94
Catbrier, 132
Catmint, 152, 155
Cedar, red-, 153
Cercidiphyllum, 43
Cercis, 44
Cerostigma. *See* Plumbago
Cherry, 41, 139, 161
Cherry-laurel, 61
Chervil, 126
Chinese date, 139
Chinese elm, 38, 39, 158
Chionanthus, 41
Chionodoxa. *See* Glory-of-the-snow
Chives, 103, 125, 126, 127, *128*
Chlordane, pesticide, 104
Choisya, 62
Christmas fern, 33, 133, 153
Christmas-rose, 124, 147
Chrysanthemum, 86, 88, 93, 108, 109, 155, 156, 158
Citrus, 88
City garden, 91-93, *150*
Cladrastis, 45
Clematis, 65, 67
Cleome, 152
Clethra, 132
Clivia, 90
Coleus, 108, 124
Colocasia, 88, 124

Index   167

Color: annuals and summer bulbs for, 114-15; berries for, 57; combination planting for, 151-63; perennials for, 109-12; for shaded areas, 124; shrubs for, 54, 56; spring-flowering bulbs for, *106, 119;* from spring to fall, 113-14
Colorado potato beetle, 103
Columbine, 133
Compost, 100
Concrete, for patio paving, 79
Concrete blocks, 79
Conifers, 37, 144-46, 152, 158
Container gardening, 86, 93, 160, *161;* plants for, 86-91; vegetables and herbs for, 136-37
Convallaria. See Lily-of-the-valley
Cordyline. See Dracena
Cork-tree. *See* Amur cork-tree
Cornus. See Dogwood
Coronilla, 33
Cosmos, 108, 116
Crabapple, flowering, 41, 73, 83, 88, 151, 159
Crabgrass control, 28
Crataegus. See Hawthorn
Crocus, 93, 105, 118-19, *121,* 122, 155
Crown-vetch, 33
Cucumber, 136, 137
Cucumber beetle, 103

Daffodil, 93, 101, 105, 118, 119-20, 122, 134, 151, 157, 159, 160
Dahlia, 105
Daisy. *See* English daisy; Marguerite; Shasta daisy
Date, Chinese, 130
Davidia, 39
Dawn-redwood, 38, 39
Day-lily, 11, 33, 100, 108, 109, 111, 112, 122, 124, 151, 152, 163
Dead-nettle, 33
Deck, *78, 79, 82,* 83
Delonix, 44
Delphinium, 101, 163
Dianthus, 111. *See also* Sweet William
Dill, 103
Dogwood, 41, *42,* 43, 148, 151, 153
Doom, disease spores, 104
Doorways, 71
Doronicum, 118
Dove tree, 39
Dracena, 88
Dryopteris, 153
Dumbarton Oaks pot garden, *89*
Dusty miller, 155

Echeveria, 155
Echinops. See Globe-thistle
Elaeagnus. See Russian-olive
Elephant's-ear, 88, 124
Elm. *See* Chinese elm
English daisy, 121
English ivy, 29, 33, 67, 93, 124, 158
Enkianthus, 161
Entrances, 71, 150
Epaulette-tree, 39
Epimedium. See Barrenwort

Erica. See Heath
Eryngium, 163
Espalier, *64,* 65
Euonymus, 36, 49, 72, 159, 160. *See also* Spindle-tree; Wintercreeper
Evergreens, 149, 151; bonsai, *154;* broad-leaved, 46-51, 147, 159; coniferous, 37, 144-46, 152, 158; dwarf, 149, 153
Evodia, 40

Fairfax Biological Laboratories, 104
Fatsia, 88
Fences, *58, 59, 64, 66, 76, 84, 92,* 151, *155*
Ferns, 88, 124, 133, 152, 153; Christmas, 33, 153
Fertilizing, 26, 28, 100, 103
Fescues, 24, 32
Festuca, 32
Field Guide to Rocky Mountain Wildflowers, A (Craighead, Craighead and Davis), 131
Field Guide to Wildflowers of Northeastern and North-central North America, A (Peterson and McKenny), 131
Fig-marigold, 33
Firethorn, 64, 88
Flagstone, 80-81
Fleecevine, dwarf, 35
Flower garden, 107-99, *110,* 151
Flowering ash, 41
Flowering onion, 120
Flowering tobacco, 116, 118
Flowering trees and shrubs. *See* under name of tree
Foamflower, 133, 153
Forsythia, 64, 159, 161
Foundation planting, *6,* 69-72, 159
Franklinia, 41
Fraxinus, 41
Fringe-tree, 41
Fruit trees, 105; dwarf, 37, 139, *140;* flowering, 41, 73, 83
Fuchsia, 108, 124

Gaillardia, 160
Galanthus. See Snowdrop
Gardenia, 88
Gardens. *See* under type of garden
Gentian, 133
Geranium, 32, 88, 93, 103, 115, 152, *157,* 161
Germander, 60
Ginkgo, 94
Gleditsia. See Honey-locust
Globe-thistle, 152, 163
Glory-of-the-snow, 117, 118, 120, 122, 155, 160
Gold-dust tree, 89
Golden-chain tree, 38, 41, 74, 83, 89
Golden-rain tree, 38, 41
Goutweed, 33
Grape-holly, 33, 46, 50-51
Grape-hyacinth, 118, 152, 155
Grasses, 23-25
Ground covers, 11, *12,* 13, 22-23, 32-36, 71-72, 93, 101
Ground-hemlock, 36
Gypsy moth, 101-2

168   Landscaping and the Small Garden

Halesia, 44
Hamamelis. See Witch-hazel
Hardy-orange, 155
Haw. See Black haw
Hawthorn, 42, 74, 159
Heath, 34, *144, 145, 146,* 147, *148,* 163
Heather, 34, *145, 146*
Hedera. See English ivy
Hedges, 5, 59-63, 152, *156*
Hemerocallis. See Day-lily
Hemlock, 37, 61, 146; ground-, 36
Herb garden, 125-30, 138, 160
Hesperis, 152
Holly, *42,* 43, 47, 50, 61, 89, 105, 124; Japanese, 94, 146-47
Holly, grape-. See Grape-holly
Holly, sea-, 163
Honey-locust, 38, 43
Honeysuckle, 34, 61, 64, 67-68, 159
Hop-tree, 43
Hosta, 11, 34, 124, 134, 151, 153
Humus, 152
Hyacinth, *80,* 93, 105, 120-21, 160
Hyacinth, grape-. See Grape-hyacinth
Hydrangea, 90, 132; climbing, 67
Hypericum, 35

Ice plant, 33
Ilex. See Holly
Impatiens, 32, 108, 115, 116, 118, 124, 159
Inchworms, 101
Insecticides, 102
Ipomoea. See Morning-glory
Iris, *81,* 109, 112, 160
Ivy, *12, 31.* See also Boston-ivy; English ivy

Jacaranda, 43
Jack-in-the-pulpit, 133
Japanese beetle, 104
Japanese spurge, 29
Jasmine, winter, 64
Jonquil. See Daffodil
Jujube, 139
Juniper, *12,* 31, 34, 63, 65, 72, 90, 151, 152, 153, 157, 158
Juniperus, 34, 90, 153

Kafir-lily, 90
Kalmia. See Mountain-laurel
Katsura-tree, 43
Kerria, 65, 163
Keukenhof Gardens, 117, 118
Kniphofia, 152
Knot garden, 125, 130
Kochia, 152
Koelreuteria. See Golden-rain tree

Laburnum. See Golden-chain tree
Ladybugs, 103, 104
Lady fern, 153
Lamb's-ears, 162
Lamium. See Archangel; Dead-nettle
Landscape architects, 19-20
Landscaping, 4-6; basic guidelines for, 18-19
Lantana, 90

Larch, 38
Lathyrus, 69
Laurus, 91
Lavender, 125, 126
Lavender-cotton, 60
Lawn, 5, 19, 21-29; grasses for, 23-25; mowing, 27-28, 97; soil preparation for, 25-26
Lawn dyes, 24-25
Lawn sods (sprigs), 24, 29
Leaf-miners, 102
Leaf mold, 100.
Lemon-verbena, 90, 126
Leopardbane, 118
Leucojum, 122
Leucothoë, 124
Liatris, 122
Ligustrum. See Privet
Lilac, 45, 163
Lilium, 121-22
Lily, 105, 121-22. See also Day-lily; Kafir-lily; Plantain-lily
Lily-of-the-Nile, 87
Lily-of-the-valley, 34, 124
Lilyturf, 34
Limestone, 26, 28
Lindera, 161
Lippia. See Lemon-verbena
Liriope, 34
Lobelia, 32, 133, 152, 159
Lobularia. See Sweet-alyssum
Lonicera. See Honeysuckle
Lupine, *81,* 108

Magnolia, 44, 74; star, 45, 94, 148, 155
Mahonia. See Grape-holly
Maidenhair fern, 133
Maidenhair tree, 94
Maintenance, 11-13, 17, 97, 111
Malathion, pesticide, 102
Malus. See Crabapple
Maple, 39, 43, 44, 45
Marginal wood fern, 153
Marguerite, 90
Marigold, 93, 103, 108, *110,* 111, 115, 116, 152, 155, 160; dwarf, 32, 155, 159
May apple, 133
Mealybugs, 103
Mertensia, 133
Mesembryanthemum, 33
Metasequoia. See Dawn-redwood
Methoxychlor, pesticide, 102
Mexican bean beetles, 103
Mexican-orange, 62
Mice, 104-5, 122, 124
Milky spore disease, 104
Mimosa, 83
Mint, 126, 130
Mock-orange, 155, 156, 161
Moles, 104
Mondo-grass, 34
Monkshood, 156
Morning-glory, 68
Moss pink, 35
Mountain-ash, 43, 83
Mountain-laurel, 9, 51, 62

Index 169

Mowing, 27-28, 97
Mugho pine, 31, 90, 151, 152, 153
Mulches and mulching, 11-12, 51, 99-100
Myrtle, 23, *30*, 35, 93, 124, 151
Myrtle, true, 126
Myrtus, 126

Narcissus. *See* Daffodil
Nasturtium, 32, 116
Nematodes, 103
Nepeta. See Catmint
Nerium, 90
Nicotiana, 116
Nicotine sulfate, 102
Norfolk Island-pine, 90
Nurseries, 19-20

Oak, 37, 39; willow, 38, 45
Oleander, 90
Ophiopogon, 34
Orchid-tree, 43
Oregano, 126
Organic gardening, 103-5, 134
Oriental poppy, 109
Osmunda, 133
Oxydendron, 44

Pachistima, 35
Pachysandra, 23, 29, 35, 72, 93, 124
Pansy, 157, 158
Park, George W., Seed Company, 159
Parrotia, 44
Parsley, 126, 128-29
Parthenocissus. See Boston-ivy; Virginia-creeper
Passiflora, 68
Passion-flower, 68
Paths, 16-17
Patio. *See* Terrace
Paxistima, 35
Peach, dwarf, 83, 139, *140*
Peach-tree borer, 103
Pear, dwarf, 139
Peat moss, 26, 100, 152, 153
Pelargonium. See Geranium
Peony, 109
Perennials, 108, 109-12, 152, 156
Periwinkle, 29, *30*, 35, 108, 124, 158, 159
Persea, 86
Pest control, 101-3, 104
Petunia, *80*, 93, 108, 111, 115, 116, 118, 152, 157, 158, 159, 162
Phellodendron. See Amur cork-tree
Philadelphus. See Mock-orange
Phlox, 35, 108, 109, 111, 122, 152; blue, 118, 123, 124
Picea. See Spruce
Picture window, 72-74
Pieris. See Andromeda
Pine, 12, 38; mugho, 31, 90, 151, 152, 153; Norfolk Island-, 90
Pine bark mulch, 100, 153
Pinus. See Pine
Pittosporum, 62
Plantain-lily, 134, 152
Planters, 83-86. *See also* Container gardening

Plum, dwarf, 139
Plumbago, 35, 156, 158
Podocarpus, 91
Podophyllum, 133
Polygonatum, 133
Polygonum, 35, 69
Polystichum. See Christmas fern
Poncirus, 155
Pools, 140-42
Poplar, 38, 94
Poppy, Oriental, 109
Portulaca, 32
Potentilla, 157
Pot garden. *See* Container gardening
Praying mantis, 103-4
Primrose, 111, 118, 121, 133, 152
Primula, 118
Privet, 59, 62, 90, 156
Ptelea, 43
Pterostyrax, 39
Puschkinia, 122, 155
Pyracantha, 158. *See also* Firethorn
Pyrethrum, pesticide, 102

Quercus. See Oak

Rabbits, 105
Railroad ties, *15, 73*
Redbud, 44
Red-cedar, 153
Redhot poker, 152
Redwood, Dawn-, 38, 39
Retaining walls, 9, *10, 15*
Rhamnus, 61
Rhododendron, 9, 46, 51, 52-54, 86, 94, 124, *144, 146,* 159
Rhubarb, 140
Rock garden, 9, *10*
Rose, 34, 62, 90, 103, 124, 147; climbing, *64,* 67; hybrid tea, 101, 105; sweetbrier, 155, 161
Rose garden, 142-43, 153
Rosemary, 91, 125, 126
Rose-of-Sharon, 158, 161
Rotenone, pesticide, 102
Royal poinciana, 44
Russian-olive, 62, 83, 94
Rye grasses, 24

Sage, 109, 126, 130
St. Johnswort, 35
Salix. See Willow
Salria, 109
Santolina, 10, 60, 126, 155
Sanvitalia. See Zinnia, creeping
Savory, 126
Scilla, 117, 118, 122, 155, 160
Sea-holly, 163
Sedum, 35, 151
Serviceberry, 44
Sevin (carbaryl), insecticide, 102
Shadblow, 44, *129*
Shadbush, 44
Shallot, 105
Shasta daisy, 111, 122

170 Landscaping and the Small Garden

Shrubs, 46, 54-57, 150, 151, 156, 157, 159-60, 161, 163
Silk-tree, 44, 83
Silverbell, 44
Silver-lace vine, 69
Skimmia, 47, 54, 147, 159
Skunk cabbage, 133
Slugs, 103
Smilacina, 133
Smoketree, 74
Snapdragon, 116, 157
Snowbell, 43
Snowdrop, 122, 155
Snowflake, 122
Soil testing kits, 23
Solomon's seal, 133
Sorbus. See Mountain-ash
Sourwood, 44
Spanish bayonet, 91
Spectricide (diazinon), pesticide, 102
Spice-bush, 161
Spiderflower, 152
Spindle-tree, 45, 160
Spirea, 159, 163
Sprays and spraying, 101-3
Spruce, dwarf Alberta, 88
Squill. *See* Scilla
Stachys, 162
State agricultural experiment stations, 19
Stewartia, 45
Stinkbugs, 103
Stonecrop, 35
Styrax, 43
Succulents, 8, 155, 161, *162*
Summer-cypress, 152
Summersweet, 132
Sweet-alyssum, 32, *80,* 107, 108, 117, 153, 155, 157, 158, 159
Sweet bay, 91
Sweet marjoram, 126
Sweet-pea, 69
Sweet rocket, 152
Sweet William, 161, 162
Sweet woodruff, 159
Swimming pools, 15-16
Symplocarpus, 133
Syringa. See Lilac
Systemics, 102

Tagetes. See Marigold
Tanbark, 81, 100
Tarragon, 126
Taxus. See Yew
Terrace, *10, 22, 40,* 75-95, 151, 152; 153, 157, 158, 160; plants for, 65, 86-91
Teucrium, 60
Thuja. See Arborvitae
Thyme, 22, 35, *123*
Tiarella, 133, 153

Tomato, 134, *136*
Tool storage house, 97-98
Tools, 81, 98-99
Tree-of-heaven, 38, 45, 93
Trees, 3-4; shade, 39-45; small, 36-39. *See also* Fruit trees
Trillium, 133
Tropaeolum. See Nasturtium
Trumpet-vine, 64
Tsuga. See Hemlock
Tub culture. *See* Container gardening
Tuberous-rooted begonia, 108, 124, 153, 159
Tulip, 93, 105, *106,* 118, *119* 121, 123-24, 151, 158, 160
Turf, for instant lawn, 29

Ulmus. See Chinese elm
Underground sprinkling system, 100
U. S. Department of Agriculture, 19

Vegetables, 134-38
Viburnum, 39, 155
Vinca. See Myrtle; **Periwinkle**
Vines, 63-69
Viola, 111
Virginia bluebells, 133
Virginia-creeper, 64, 67, 132
Virgin's-bower, 65
Vitex, 158-59

Walks, 16-17
Water garden, 140
Wax begonia, 32, 108, 124, 151, 159
Weed control, 28
Weevils, 103
Wild-flower garden, 101, 130-34, 152
Willow, 38, 74, 91, 94; arctic, 155, 156
Willow-oak, 38, 45
Window boxes, 94-95
Wintercreeper, 36, 49, 69, 124
Winter garden effects, 143-48
Wisteria, 64, 65, *66,* 158
Witch-hazel, 147, 153
Wood chips, 81, 100
Woodland garden, 9, *47,* 101, *129,* 130-31; native plants for, 132 133

Xanthoceras, 45

Yellow-horn, 45
Yellow-wood, 45
Yew, 36, 63, 65, 72, 74, 91, 151, *156* 158; podocarpus, 91
Yucca, 91

Zinnia, 108, *110,* 115, 117; creeping, 32, 160; dwarf, 32, 152, *156,* 159, 160, 162
Zizyphus, 139
Zoysia grass, 24, 25